HAUNTED HILLS AND HOLLOWS

What Lurks in Greene County, Pennsylvania

HAUNTED HILLS AND HOLLOWS

What Lurks in Greene County, Pennsylvania

Rosemary Ellen Guiley
and
Kevin Paul

Visionary Living Publishing/Visionary Living, Inc.
New Milford, Connecticut

Haunted Hills and Hollows:
What Lurks in Greene County, Pennsylvania

By Rosemary Ellen Guiley and Kevin Paul

Copyright Rosemary Ellen Guiley and Kevin Paul, 2018

Front cover design by April Slaughter
Back cover and interior design by Leslie McAllister

ISBN: 978-1-942157-31-1 (pbk)
ISBN: 978-1-942157-32-8 (epub)

Published by Visionary Living Publishing/Visionary Living, Inc.
New Milford, Connecticut
www.visionarylivingpublishing.com

TABLE OF CONTENTS

Acknowledgments
Kevin Paul

My heartfelt thanks and appreciation to the following people, for without their patience, support, expertise and encouragement this book would never have come into being:

Amy Paul: my wife, best friend, and partner for life.

Morgan Paul: who is always ready to see what's behind the next door and rarely panics when she does.

Benjamin Paul and Euphen Scott: for teaching me to look twice and how to think outside the box.

Rosemary Ellen Guiley: mentor, adviser and friend.

Stan Gordon: western Pennsylvania's go-to guy for unexplained events.

Thanks to Visionary Living Publishing, John Zaffis, Peter Davenport, Lon Strickler, Dakota Corwin, Karen Romah, Shorty Waychoff, Chelsea Hillberry, John Weaver, Laume Conroy, David Weatherly and anyone inadvertently omitted.

Special thanks to the dozens of Greene County residents who willingly shared their experiences, thoughts and fears about what may still be prowling about the countryside just at the very edge of our senses' ability to detect them.

Preface

In 2010, after an appearance on *Coast to Coast AM* with George Noory, I received an email from Kevin Paul inviting me to come to Greene County, Pennsylvania, where I would not be disappointed by all the strange paranormal activity taking place there. I receive many emails like this, especially after a big radio show, and most of them don't measure up to the billing. Something about this one gave me pause. Call it a hunch, good old-fashioned gut instinct, intuition or a bolt from the gods – I knew I needed to follow up.

From my very first trip to Greene County, I was amazed by the paranormal goings on. There were phenomena aplenty in this southwestern corner of the Keystone State. Its hills and hollows held many mysteries; the skies were full of unexplained lights and craft; the houses and buildings teemed with all kinds of ghosts and spirits; odd entities and "people" drifted over the landscape. The land itself held an eerie energy. I've investigated in countless places around the US and even internationally, including many famous places that grab the spotlight. Mile for square mile, Greene County packs quite a paranormal punch, more than some of those famous places.

After that first trip, I was hooked, and many more trips to Greene County followed over the years. I met many experiencers and received more invitations to investigate places. A wonderful friendship developed with Kevin and his family. We started discussing this book, and spent several years pulling it together. Along the way, both of us were plagued by odd phenomena and trickster experiences, the likes of which happen to many paranormal researchers: missing files, phone messages that go into oblivion, malfunctioning computers and phones, odd apports (relocated objects), and so on.

As a lifelong resident of Greene County, Kevin knows all of its secret nooks and crannies, and what supernatural things have happened, where and when. Kevin has done the bulk of the sleuthing and writing for this book, and so when you see the first-person pronoun "I," that's Kevin talking.

I know you will enjoy *Haunted Hills and Hollows: What Lurks in Greene County, Pennsylvania*. It's perfect for late night reading – with a flashlight!

– Rosemary Ellen Guiley

INTRODUCTION

Greene County was carved out of what seemed to be a vast unending wilderness by an act of the Pennsylvania Legislature on February 9, 1796. America was a new country; the sky was the limit. History was waiting to be written.

Along with the history that would fill the schoolbooks of children came another history as well, one not spoken of openly: the supernatural and paranormal.

Greene County was named after Revolutionary War hero Nathanael Greene. Its original European settlers consisted of immigrants of German, Irish, Scotch, Scotch-Irish and English origin. Native to the region, and at times at war with the European invaders, were members of the Sachem Six Nations, also known as the Iroquois Confederacy. They included the Mohawk, Oneida, Onondaga, Cayuga, Seneca and Tuscarora Indians.

It should come as no surprise that when the white settlers arrived in numbers that there would be inevitable friction between those of European descent and the native inhabitants. In fact, one historical account claimed in 1888 that the "section of the country, of which Greene County occupies a central position, has more vitally interesting problems in its history than any other portion of the United States." That may or may not have been the case, but that statement certainly puts an interesting spin on the corner of Pennsylvania where locals often lament that nothing noteworthy, past or present, ever occurs in Greene County.

There is no doubt that some events of historical significance took place here in the very early days. There were significant altercations between the pioneer families and their Native American neighbors that resulted in a lot of bloodshed. Some have claimed that the Indians never established permanent settlements in this part of Pennsylvania, preferring to use it as a sort of game reserve for hunting and supplying the native population. Thus, the inevitable clash between whites and natives arose as a result of the settlers' axe work and farming that interfered with the natives' hunting and occasional war parties traversing both the Warrior and Catawba Trails.

And clash they did: oral and written histories of the county make mention of the fighting between the peoples of both races for many years. One historian stated that, "Probably no equal portion of any part of the United States has been the scene of so many cold-blooded and heartless murders by the Indians as this county; not because the pioneers here provoked the natives to revenge, nor because they were special objects of hatred, but because they happened to be in the way..." Many local residents descended from the original white settlers of Greene County (in my case the Rineharts of the Coal Lick Creek watershed in Franklin Township) have heard and read of the savagery of the fighting. Fortunately, enough time has passed for us to realize that there were scoundrels on both sides, and not all the butchery was the fault of the indigenous people.

Fast forward through the 18th, 19th and 20th centuries to the 21st century. The exploitation of the Indians was gradually replaced by agriculture and extraction industries associated with the Industrial Revolution. Timber, coal, oil and natural gas have all been harvested here in great quantities, and, thanks to technology, on a greater and more efficient scale.

What does this very brief history have to do with a book on the paranormal in Greene County? Believers and non-believers alike flock to places like Gettysburg, Harpers Ferry, Weston, Point Pleasant, Moundsville, and Salem to experience the hauntings arising from the rich histories of those places (battles, abolitionists, lunatic asylums, bridge collapses, prisons, Native American mounds, witch trials and more). The incredible volume of human emotion generated then reverberates through the ages and can still be felt today.

Greene County shares many characteristics with better-known paranormal hot spots. Just like Gettysburg, Moundsville, or Salem, it has a bloody, albeit not as well-known, history. Many paranormal researchers have linked violence and human anguish with unexplained activities, and our own history, sadly, is rich in both. We could not stake our claim as the "Most Haunted County in America" without taking into account tales of the massacres and mayhem of our distant and not so distant past, which took place on the hills and in the hollows frequented by dogmen, UFOs, Bigfoot, spectral dogs, ghosts, demonic beings and a host of other entities that quite often do far more than go bump in the proverbial night.

It is important to note that many of the locations mentioned in this book are on private property and that the authors in no way encourage or endorse trespassing for any reason. We have, by request, disguised some identities and exact locations.

Much of what is recognized as paranormal activity consists of phenomena that have been recorded by societies all over the world. Sasquatch, the Yeti and Bigfoot bear a striking resemblance to each other. Ghostly encounters have been recorded all over the world, but the ghosts themselves share common characteristics and behaviors. The troublesome Pukwudgies of New England have similarities to trolls, and fairies share their stage with pixies, elves, imps and leprechauns. While entities' traits may be similar all over the world, only their names change.

We've placed activities by locales, but keep in mind that residents of the supernatural realm do not pay any attention to the lines drawn on maps by human beings.

– Kevin Paul

Chapter 1

The Lobster Alien and Other Strange Beings

It is not unusual for many unexplained things to haunt isolated landscapes, as residents of the more remote parts of Greene County discover. Families stay in areas and even the same houses for generations, and individuals grow accustomed to the things and spirits that share the land with them. Even new residents quickly find out that the land holds a peculiar energy and many strange and disturbing phenomena. Learn to live with them – or leave.

Growing up haunted

Sherry (not her real name) grew up as an only child with her parents in such an area. At night, black shadow figures flitted around the barn, and the little gray scurrying things, creatures of unknown origin, zipped over the land as well. Occasionally the quiet of the night would be pierced with the blood-curdling screams of Sasquatch. Large footprints that could not be explained were sometimes found. Not animal, not human, not even Sasquatch, they might have been made by dogmen. They were longer and bigger than a human print, smaller than most Sasquatch prints – and featured long claws three to four inches in length. In addition, black spectral dogs made frequent appearances at a certain bend in the road nearby.

Frequently, Sherry would wake up in the middle of the night to see a gray-to-black figure standing at the foot of the bed, as though it were watching her. Sometimes it would vanish as soon as she saw it, and sometimes it would remain planted on the spot for some time before it disappeared. The figure would either just disappear or would go out through the glass window.

When the figure was gray, it resembled a gray alien with large, slanted black eyes. When the figure was black, it was more humanoid in shape, and looked as though it were wearing a large overcoat and a hat. Sometimes Sherry could see round eyes.

Telling her mother about the figure got only a dismissal: it was either aliens or one of her departed grandparents, and in either case, it was "looking in on her."

Most strange of all was the aerial activity – what Sherry's mother explained away as "just the aliens looking in on us." In the late 1960s and into the 1970s, bright lights that were like searchlights illuminated the hill behind the house, and sometimes the entire valley. Bright lights would shine in Sherry's second-floor bedroom window. A few times, she glimpsed craft in the nighttime sky – triangular with lights on the underneath, and disc-shaped with rotating multi-colored lights on the rim.

Sherry's unusual experiences began early in life. She shared a gift with her mother of a sensitivity to the paranormal. Her father was a disbeliever. Her mother was never frightened by anything that happened in and around the family home, and so Sherry was never frightened either.

The mystery veil

Sherry discovered that there was a peculiar force field on the hill outside the house. The hill possessed an unsettling energy, and it was marked by small "igloos" carefully made of stone. No one knew who made the igloos or why, but Sherry felt they should remain undisturbed.

She would go walking on the hill with her dog, and part way up, where the igloos were located, she would run into what she called a "veil." It was like a fog. If she entered it, she lost all memory until she returned to the house. She had no idea if the dog came with her. According to her mother, she would be absent for about an hour.

Sherry never had any recollection of what happened to her once she entered the fog.

One of the curious stone igloos behind "the veil." Credit: R.E. Guiley.

Attempted abduction by a lobster-thing

When Sherry was 14, she had an alarming experience that might have been a botched alien abduction. She "woke up" to find herself dangling by one arm in the claw of a huge creature that resembled a crayfish or a lobster. It had enormous antennae and was about seven to eight feet tall. The creature was in the window, which was missing its glass and appeared to have become a doorway that was strangely lit.

The creature was attempting to extract her through the window area. Sherry struggled against it, and it dropped her to the floor.

The next thing she knew, Sherry was awake in the morning lying on her side on the floor. Her shoulder ached mightily, and she had a huge black and blue bruise on the arm where the creature had taken hold of her.

At first, Sherry thought she had dreamed the experience – but she could not explain how she had landed on the floor, why her shoulder hurt, and why she had a massive bruise below the elbow.

The experience, which took place in the late 1970s, sounds like a B-grade science fiction movie sporting giant insect-like aliens. Do aliens really look like giant lobsters – or do we see what we are able to see when we look upon a form we do not comprehend?

Sherry has memories of being taken aboard alien ships at about the same time and being in rooms where she saw surgical-type tools or instruments and gray aliens. She had no recollection of being probed like other abductees or experiencing any pain.

Now that Sherry is older, her alien experiences have come to an end. This follows a pattern observed by abduction researchers: experiences begin early in life, may involve more than one family member, and sometimes come to an end when the person reaches adulthood.

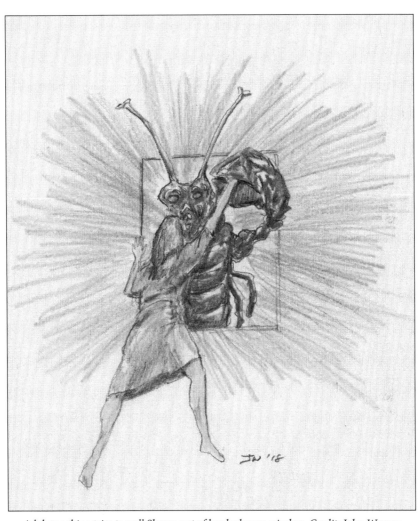

A lobster-thing tries to pull Sherry out of her bedroom window. Credit: John Weaver.

Return of Sasquatch

In July of 2017 Sherry noticed the return of the howling Sasquatch, usually in conjunction with a waxing and nearly full moon, although not every month. When it first returned, it seemed to prefer the wooded area where the veil exists. At times the creature has been quite close to the house as it screams and spooks their livestock.

Falling stars

Sherry also has seen what she thought were meteors falling to earth. The first, in August of 2014, had a bright white tail, and like the UFOs of her youth, it lit up the valley. She witnessed the second in early October 2017; oddly enough around 9:30 PM, about the time she hears the screaming. The object fell from the sky with a loud boom and left a sparkling visible trail that she observed for nearly five minutes. From Sherry's vantage point it seemed to hit the ground, similar to a six-foot chunk of asteroid or comet debris that fell to earth in Michigan in January 2018. The Michigan event had a long-lasting tail as well, resembling what Sherry saw.

Sherry continues to experience the haunting phenomena that roams the land of her native area. These things never go away.

Other witnesses

Sherry is not alone in witnessing odd happenings in her corner of Greene County. Another witness, Jill (not her real name) grew up very close to Sherry's farm. She too witnessed black shadowy figures and small scurrying things outside their home. She came to dread being asked by her parents to feed the dogs outside in the evening as the scurrying entities would dash about, as if they were attracted to her movement. She has heard the screaming as well, often close to her former home. Whenever it happened, their dogs became very agitated, barking and growling loudly as the screams' echoes faded.

Jill also saw a UFO very similar to that seen by Sherry, but their sightings are 30 years apart. She reported seeing a disc-shaped object with red, green and blue lights moving silently just above the trees about 500 yards from her bedroom window. She was able to observe the object rotating for several minutes before it vanished. Perhaps the most interesting aspect of Sherry's and Jill's reports is the fact that neither knew of the other's sightings, yet they seemed to be witnessing the same phenomenon.

Ghost boy in the road

Jill also relayed another disturbing encounter involving the specter of a small boy. She was driving home one day when a young boy, perhaps three years of age and with blond hair, climbed the guardrail and darted into the road in front of her. She immediately swerved into the path of an oncoming vehicle and the two narrowly avoided a head-on collision. Jumping out of her car, she looked to see where the child was and could not locate him. The driver of the other vehicle approached her, asked if she were okay and inquired what had made her cut in front of him. She replied she took action to avoid hitting the child, who should have been in plain sight of the other driver. Both he and his passenger saw nothing, telling her there was no child in the road.

A huge cryptid

Another report comes from a contractor employed by an agency of the federal government working in the area during the summer of 2017. Phillip (not his real name) was driving past Jill's former residence toward Sherry's farm. Phillip reported that he was driving down a narrow country road through a wooded area that is intersected by a natural gas pipeline. For maintenance purposes, the gas line is cleared periodically of brush and trees. As was his habit, Phillip looked at the gas line right-of-way hoping to spot some wildlife. What he saw was a large animal walking from left to right in the clearing. It was brown and furry, and he guessed its weight at 400-500 pounds.

He stopped his truck to observe what he thought was a bear. The animal, however, was walking on two feet, and upon hearing the vehicle it crouched down in the brush. Phillip waited and could make out movement in the vegetation; evidently the animal was down on all fours in an effort to exit the clearing unobserved. It reached the edge of the woods and Phillip lost sight of it.

He waited a few moments longer and the creature peered out from behind a tree, its head perhaps seven feet off the ground. Phillip realized that he might not be watching a bear, a thought that was confirmed when the creature reached around the trunk of the tree with a long arm as if to steady itself. Was this Bigfoot, or some other cryptid? Phillip, shaken by the encounter, chose not to investigate further and drove off.

CHAPTER 2

MASSACRES: BLOOD-SOAKED GROUND

The paranormal activity in Greene County has a legacy of violence going back to the days of colonial America, when tensions between colonists and natives led to massacres of both sides. According to one historian, an astonishing 100 massacres took place within the confines of modern-day Greene County, literally soaking the landscape in blood.

Locations where bloody violence and death have occurred, such as battlefields and mass murder, often become heavily haunted. Ghostly residues of the violence linger as apparitional visions, sounds, smells and poltergeist activity, sometimes for centuries. The bloodshed of massacres also energizes the ground in peculiar ways, perhaps creating or contributing to ideal conditions for the fertile feeding grounds of mysterious beings. Homes, buildings and farms on or even near such sites can be afflicted with a wide range of paranormal activity.

Peace gives way to violence

There's a curious and intriguing contradiction regarding just who lived in what is now Greene County prior to the arrival of people of European descent. It is known that the Monongahela Indians inhabited this region, and some accounts make reference to the Iroquois, Algonquin, Seneca and Lenape (also known as Delaware) as well. Most accounts state that the Monongahela were one of the earliest, followed by the others. As the whites arrived and the French and Indian War (1754-1763) was getting under way, the Shawnee, Lenape, Mingo and Wyandot stopped the western progress of the expanding, soon-to-be states by standing firm with their backs to the Ohio River for more than 50 years. Those of European descent were intent on forcing the native population west of the river and beyond.

According to contemporary accounts, there were peaceful relations between the first Europeans to settle in the area and their Native American counterparts. One such person was Thomas Slater, who once owned the tract on which the Borough of Waynesburg now stands. Mr. Slater was known to be "on terms of intimacy with the Indians and was accustomed to receiving them in a most friendly manner, pitching quoits (similar to pitching horseshoes), running, leaping, and shooting at mark with them." We will hear more about Thomas Slater later in this book.

As white settlers came in increasing numbers and took over more land, tensions rose with the Native Americans. Skirmishes became more frequent and were violent and bloody. There were many clashes between the two cultures referred to as massacres by the whites, who eventually prevailed over the indigenous people. While many of the massacres were well documented in historical texts and newspapers, the exact cause of the bloodshed is frequently glossed over by referencing the alleged treachery and barbarous nature of Indian civilization. It is probably safe to say that any acts of the Native Americans deemed inappropriate were no doubt matched and at times surpassed by those of the invading settlers.

Logan's revenge

Peaceful relations between settlers and natives ended about the time of the Yellow Creek massacre (in present day Hancock County, West Virginia) in 1774. A band of 32 whites butchered and scalped the family of Logan, including his pregnant wife. Logan was one of 10 Iroquois council chiefs who "up to that time was known as the 'white man's friend.'" Following the massacre of his family, Logan, according to one description, "was transformed into an avenging demon. His name became a terror. At his beck and call, settlements disappeared with a 'besom of destruction.' The soil of Greene County drank the blood of almost numberless victims to his power. Well could reeking scalps, vacant hearths and smoldering ruins attest his boast: 'I have sought revenge. I have killed many. I have fully glutted my vengeance.'"

Chief Logan. Credit: Ohio Historical Society.

Logan's avenging sweep through Greene County helped to ignite Lord Dunmore's War, culminating in the Battle of Point Pleasant, West Virginia, where he dictated Logan's Lament following the Indians' defeat at the hands of Colonel Andrew Lewis.

The Spicer massacre

Let us first examine the unhappy fate of the Spicer family, who once lived in what is now Greene Township. While their name is still known, the exact location of their homestead is lost. Some believe it was somewhere on the ridge top that separates Dunkard Creek from Whiteley Creek, which could very well have put it very near the Warrior Trail and a portion of SR 2011, Wise Road, or Roberts Run Road. Other early historians placed the Spicer homestead in the vicinity of Willow Tree or Bobtown.

William and Lydia Spicer and their seven children (some accounts state they had five) had established themselves in a small cabin surrounded by previously undisturbed forest in the hills. They were among the first settlers to be attacked by Logan and his warriors.

As Logan's band approached the Spicer home deep in the woods, William Spicer stopped chopping wood, struck his axe into a log, and entered his cabin to prepare a welcome for the Indians. One of Logan's men took the axe and struck Spicer, his wife and two children dead inside the cabin. The speed and efficiency of the attack prevented them from offering any resistance. Three more Spicer children were quickly killed, leaving Elizabeth, who was ironing clothes, and her brother William. The pair ran for their lives, Elizabeth still holding the iron. Upon reaching a fence, she and William were captured and taken away.

The remainder of the Spicer family was scalped, and their bodies were mutilated so horrifically that the leader of a detail sent to bury the dead had to be led away.

Elizabeth and William were taken at least as far west as across the Ohio River, where Elizabeth learned to speak the natives' language as well as gain an understanding of the use of herbs, plants and roots for medicine. She and William were separated so as to lessen the likelihood of their trying to escape.

A subsequent treaty required the Indians to release their captives. Elizabeth returned to Greene County, married a man named Bowen, and gained status among her peers, thanks to her knowledge of the use of native plants as pharmaceuticals. William, on the other hand, became fully assimilated into the Indian culture in Ohio, and took a Native American wife. Eventually becoming a chief, he returned to the area at least once in order to give testimony supporting Elizabeth's claims to some property. Preferring his adopted lifestyle, William was never persuaded to leave his former captors and rejoin the white community in Greene County. According to some accounts, his name is associated with another Greene County massacre, as we shall soon see.

The Davis massacre

We will now examine the largest Indian massacre of a single family in Greene County. Early in the morning in the fall of 1787, John Davis with his wife and 10 children were going about their daily routine at their homestead (in what is now part of Ryerson Station State Park) when the eldest daughter reported seeing Indians hiding near their cabin. An attempt to grab their guns when the Indians came into their cabin proved fruitless. The eldest daughter leapt to safety through a window. Additionally, two other daughters and a grown son who were in the cabin during the commotion escaped.

Seven members of the family lost their lives inside the cabin: John Davis, his two oldest sons and four younger children. Mrs. Davis and a baby daughter were taken captive. The fate of Mrs. Davis was never established, but the body of the baby girl was found some weeks later. Although her body was never found, it is assumed that Mrs. Davis also perished at the time, bringing the total of this tragedy to nine victims, all of whom now share an unmarked common grave.

Even though this was the worst massacre of a single family in Greene County history, other massacres such as those of the Corbly and Crow families are better documented, and as a result better known.

The John Davis house from an early drawing. The house no longer exists.

During the 1780s, Garard's Fort was established in Whiteley Township approximately where a current village bears the same name. Strategically situated near Whiteley Creek, Garard's Fort became the "go-to" place for white settlers during times of unrest and skirmishing with the Native

Marker commemorating Corbly massacre. Credit: R.E. Guiley.

Americans. On October 7, 1776 one of, if not the, first church in the county was established and it soon attracted the Reverend John Corbly to serve as pastor. On May 2, 1782 Corbly was following his family as they strolled to worship that Sunday morning. Corbly later stated he was some distance behind his wife and children, meditating with his Bible.

The serene Sunday morning was pierced by the shouts of not only attacking Indians but his family as well. Corbly, realizing his family was in danger, rushed toward them only to be warned off by his wife as she and the Corbly children were attacked without quarter. The reverend and two daughters survived. The daughters suffered from anxiety for the rest of their lives.

While frightful in its savagery, the Corbly attack was not the worst experience endured by families of white settlers. Perhaps it is better known because the victims were the wife and family of a man of the cloth whose written accounts of the incident were widely circulated in the years following the event. At present, the Corbly massacre is marked by the most elaborate monument to the sacrifice of white settlers in Greene County, likely due to its location and notoriety.

A small monument to the Davis family is set near the Ryerson Station State Park office that marks the approximate location of their demise.

The Crow massacre

About three miles from the Davis tragedy of 1787, members of the Crow family met the same fate. Four daughters of Jacob Crow: Elizabeth, Susanna, Katharine and Christina, ages ranging from 10 to 16, are said to have been returning from visiting a neighbor in early May of 1791. They were stopped at a stream when they were accosted by two Native Americans and a "heartless renegade white man by the name of (William) Spicer."

Grabbing the girls and bidding them to keep silent, the men forced them to a ravine, sat them on a fallen tree, and began to interrogate them about their homestead and its defensive capability. Initially at least, the sisters talked among themselves in their native German in order that their captors would not be able to understand them. Their interrogation was apparently fruitless, and the three men began arguing amongst themselves about the fate of their captives. There was some disagreement as to whether the girls should be killed or taken as captives back to Ohio.

16

Sadly, the decision was made to dispatch them rather than spare their lives. Susanna was killed first by an Indian, and Katharine was mortally wounded by Spicer. Christina and Elizabeth were both held by one Indian and Christina broke free. As she ran for her life, she was struck in the back by a pursuing Indian using either a tomahawk or gun muzzle and was left for dead. Miraculously, she survived.

The condition of Elizabeth's and Susanna's bodies was described as "literally butchered, mangled, dead, scalped." Katharine, also scalped, was found alive but died within days. Christina carried scars on her back for the remainder of her life.

Years later at a small celebration at the home of Jacob Crow, an Indian and a stranger stopped by, begging for food. Christina Crow, survivor of the Crow massacre, recognized the Indian and the stranger as Spicer, the murderers of her sisters. She relayed this information to her brother, Michael, and a friend of his named Dickerson. Michael and Dickerson had a brief whispered conversation outside, gathered their weapons, and gave chase.

Intent on vengeance, the two men tracked their quarry for some distance but allegedly lost their trail. They returned home, and Michael said he and Dickerson had a difficult time gaining ground on the two. While Michael claimed the chase was abandoned on the second day, Dickerson stated he and Michael had gotten close enough to Spicer and his accomplice to "count the buttons on the Indian's coat."

Some believed that Spicer and the Indian were caught and killed by Crow and Dickerson. Others believed Michael's claims that the fugitives were never caught. Local authorities, believing the hearsay that Spicer and his Indian companion were dead, had Michael Crow apprehended on suspicion of murder.

The charges were dropped due to a lack of evidence and a statement by a hunter that both Spicer and the Indian had been seen in Ohio after their alleged deaths. Michael Crow subsequently was released, but their neighbors would continue to hint and speculate that he avenged the death of his sisters. From that point forward both Michael and Dickerson remained silent about the incident.

And what of this renegade white man by the name of Spicer involved in the Crow Massacre? Some believed he was the William Spicer who had been taken captive and lived among the Indians in Ohio. Others claimed that he was not; William Spicer had become a respected and wealthy chief who maintained good relations with the whites and was poisoned by a jealous rival.

Some said it was not a man named Spicer, but instead the infamous Simon Girty, a first-class scoundrel. Girty, like Spicer, had been captured by Native Americans and assimilated well into their lifestyle. Returned to his mother following the French and Indian War, Girty became well known as an interpreter. During the Revolutionary

Rock that sheltered the Crow sisters during the massacre. Credit: Kevin Paul.

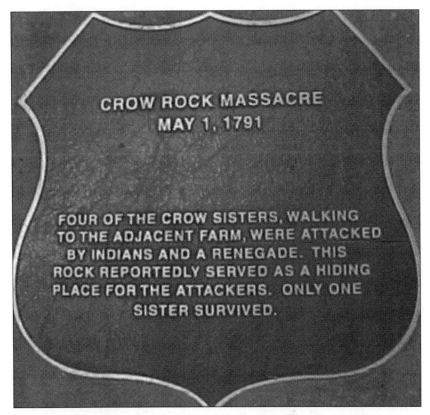

CROW ROCK MASSACRE
MAY 1, 1791

FOUR OF THE CROW SISTERS, WALKING
TO THE ADJACENT FARM, WERE ATTACKED
BY INDIANS AND A RENEGADE. THIS
ROCK REPORTEDLY SERVED AS A HIDING
PLACE FOR THE ATTACKERS. ONLY ONE
SISTER SURVIVED.

Text of stone marker comemmorating Crow massacre. Credit: Kevin Paul.

War he first sided with the Americans and chafed under their treatment, eventually going over to the British. He gained somewhat of a reputation for brutality because of reports of his refusing to shoot a white man (Colonel William Crawford) being burned at the stake by the Indians even though Crawford begged him to do so. Crawford was being punished for massacring Indians in nearby Gnadenhutten, Ohio. More modern accounts of Girty's life are somewhat kinder. He was a capable frontiersman who successfully walked the thin line between clashing civilizations, often using his status within the Native American community to plead for mercy on behalf of captured whites.

The consensus among early Greene County historians was that the renegade white man was indeed *that* William Spicer, and that he took part not only in the Crow slaughter and possibly the Davis massacre as well. At least one author reported that William Spicer was killed on the eastern side of the Ohio River, then skinned and his hide tanned into leather. That does indeed sound like the possible handiwork of an avenging brother, one Michael Crow.

A monument to the Crow massacre victims is located slightly off the beaten path in the western end of Greene County.

The paranormal connection

This violent, bloody history has left its paranormal mark upon the landscape, and over a wide territory. But were these acts just about revenge, or did they have a spiritual component as well?

The Spicers and others were dispatched by Logan and his warriors in retaliation for wrongful acts committed by whites against the native population. Records mention the political and military moves of the British and colonials following the Spicer massacre in what is known as Lord Dunmore's War. There is little or no discussion about the spiritual aspect of the clash of colonial American culture against that of the Indians. Early accounts paint the settlers as hard working, modest, devout and peaceful, while portraying Native Americans as devilish schemers lurking behind every tree waiting to pounce upon unsuspecting colonials who would mean them no harm.

Today we think that before our highways, cars and trucks, very little travel took place. Logan, who killed the Spicer family and took hostages back to Ohio, did not die in this region but was killed in Detroit. The only major battle of Lord Dunmore's War took place at what is now Point Pleasant, West Virginia, and one factor leading up to this battle was the Spicer massacre hundreds of miles to the north.

Travel did indeed take place, but on foot or horseback. Travel for commerce, hunting and exploration was common; is it not reasonable to believe travel in defense of places of spiritual importance was important as well? We know there are reports of Indian mounds at Crow's Mills not far from where the Crow sisters were slaughtered, as well as a telltale depression in the ground. Is it possible that both the Davis and Crow massacres were not the result of random acts of wanton violence, but instead an attempt to dislodge whites from areas held sacred? Both families had successfully established themselves almost in the shadow of Indian mound burial sites. It is not unfathomable to consider the possibility that both the Davis and Crow massacres were carried out in a vain attempt to defend sacred sites from desecration and destruction.

The Crow Rock Massacre Monument has not only preserved the memory of the slain sisters but also is said to be the very rock from which their attackers hid as they waited in ambush. As a result of the construction of a flood control dry dam, the monument has been moved approximately 100 feet to its present location along Crow Rock Road and is open to the public.

There have been reports of paranormal activity in this area. Motorists have reported sightings of Indians along the road in the vicinity of Crow Rock. There have also been sporadic reports of loud, bloodcurdling screams heard in the hours just before daylight at the monument itself. While conducting research for this book, I was able to access some of the original design drawings of the flood control dry dam. The drawings clearly indicate two burial mounds, and I interviewed an individual who was part of a survey team working on the project. He confirmed that there were mounds present at the work site. It is interesting to note that a review of official historical documents indicates that at least one of the mounds was of considerable length, or else the Crow Farm was home to a complex of mounds as opposed to just two.

Ryerson Station State Park, the site of the Davis massacre, has had its share of unexplained happenings as well. Years ago, the Lazear family erected the brick farmhouse that is now surrounded by the park but not part of the park that is open to the public. The house itself stands tall on a mound-like structure; contemporary maps showing the landscape contours and elevations clearly illustrate a building centered on top of a circular formation. Like the mounds at Crow's Mills, this formation is adjacent to a stream and/or in a flood plain, and it is unlikely to have been formed by nature.

During construction the Lazear family uncovered the remains of Native Americans and subsequently reinterred them nearby. The actual location of the reinterment was never revealed in order that the human remains would be undisturbed in their new resting place.

Odd happenings occur within the house: thumps and bangs, footsteps heard in unoccupied rooms and loud scraping sounds as if someone were moving furniture.

Paranormal activity near Crow Rock/Massacre site, Ryerson State Park

Amber and Arthur Geiger live in a home that, for better or worse, is located quite close to not only the Crow Massacre site but also the site of the Davis Massacre in today's Ryerson Station State Park. Both have had their share of unusual experiences.

One evening Arthur and some friends were in the Geiger garage, which is detached from the house. Amber was asleep in the house when she heard someone pecking on the window. She ignored it at first, thinking it was Arthur or one of their friends pulling a prank on her. The pecking continued, and was accompanied by a voice saying, "Help me, help me... someone help me... please help me."

By this time their dog joined in, became agitated and started to bark at the window. Amber then heard the voice say, "Help me, or else!" Irritated, and still thinking this was a prank, Amber went to the window and was startled to see the figure of a young girl with long hair running away from the house. She confronted Arthur and their friends who not only denied pulling a prank but also flatly stated there was no little girl nearby. Later that evening their bedroom radio turned itself on and played softly, then increased in volume until it was loud enough to wake the household. Then it turned itself off.

The same little girl, or perhaps another, paid a visit on at least one other occasion. Amber was cleaning house when she began to feel as if she were not alone. She thought someone was behind her and turned around to see a spectral image of a little girl of eight to nine years of age. Their dog immediately approached the figure, and she vanished.

The presence of a spectral little girl is intriguing. Both the Davis and Crow families lost young daughters to murders of almost unimaginable savagery, both of which took place within walking distance of Amber and Arthur's home. Much has been written about the untimely deaths of the Crow sisters, including their approximate ages. Of the four, Elizabeth was approximately 10 years of age. She perished at the hands of her attackers, as did two of her sisters. One sister, Katharine, survived for three days despite her wounds. One written account describes the efforts made by her family to save her life, including a hazardous 20-mile journey to Wheeling, West Virginia to get the help of a physician.

Part of her scalp was found and an attempt to reattach it failed. Her wounds were so severe that reportedly a portion of her skull was missing and assumed to be still attached to the unfound remainder of her scalp. When discovered by a search party, she is reported to have asked her brother Michael why it took so long for him to return with help.

Is it possible that after more than 225 years the ghost of Elizabeth Crow is attempting to get help for her sister Katharine who "survived in torment for three days, before being relieved by death"?

There have been other strange occurrences in the vicinity. Arthur was traveling home from work on Crow's Rock Road one evening in late 2017. He was tired and distracted by his long day and the drive. As he neared the Crow Monument he was startled by a deer darting in front of him. Hitting the brakes, he couldn't help but notice the deer seemed

23

to have been spooked by something other than his SUV and it quickly disappeared into the darkness.

Arthur drove away slowly when he noticed something along the edge of the road. As he approached the dark mass he realized that there was a dark-colored animal off the road to his left. An avid off-road enthusiast, Arthur stopped his SUV again and flipped on his auxiliary off-road lights. Much to his astonishment he made eye contact with what looked like a large gorilla just in front of him, crouching down in a squatting position and bracing itself against the ground with its hands.

The creature, perhaps agitated by the blinding off-road lights of the vehicle, moved off in the same direction as the deer. It was large, seemed to be covered by dark brown or black hair, and had bright glowing red eyes. It moved on all fours, like an ape, slowly and deliberately, staring at Arthur the entire time. The ape-like posture and movement witnessed by Arthur has been seen elsewhere in southwestern Pennsylvania and has been well documented by researcher Stan Gordon.

Upon crossing the road, it disappeared as quickly as had the deer. Arthur deftly turned the vehicle in the direction the creature had taken, hoping to catch it in the glare of his lights. While the creature managed to stay hidden, it let out a bloodcurdling scream. Arthur sped off toward home and told Amber of his encounter Within minutes the couple returned to the spot. There was no creature to be seen, but it continued to scream and howl, and there was a foul odor in the air similar to sulfur.

One of the pair's favorite activities is off-road driving. They frequent a popular spot near Nebo Ridge known for a series of mud holes, challenging both their driving skills and their vehicle by mud bogging. On more than one occasion and regardless of the season both have noticed white orb-like lights moving through the trees and just in front of their SUV. At times seeing the lights caused Amber to have a nosebleed. At other times, when taking a break from mud bogging and their vehicle is not running, both have heard what sounds like people screaming in the distance. Like other locations that play host to mysterious happenings in Greene County, this one is close to a site of well-known and documented Native American activity, in this case a village site on land now owned by the Pennsylvania Game Commission.

Bristoria Road will take today's travelers not only to Ryerson Station State Park but also past the approximate location of the Davis Massacre as well. Early one evening, Amber was taking younger members of the family to their home on Bristoria Road near the edge of the state park. Upon their arrival, her passengers were alarmed and refused to exit the vehicle, saying there were strange people in the yard. Amber could see them as well, although she denied it at the time so as not to alarm her passengers. She saw a number of people, both men and women, milling about in the yard. The women were all wearing long, flowing dresses and some of the men were wearing old-style military uniforms. When shown an unlabeled drawing of historic American military uniforms, Amber pointed to one from the years 1775-1790 as similar to what she had seen that night.

Chapter 3

Mounds and Disturbed Burials

As mentioned in the previous chapter, Native American mounds may play a role in the haunting legacy of the land. Greene County has a very rich, and sadly a little-publicized, history of mound builders.

Who were the mound builders?

Prior to the presence of the Monongahela were the Adena, or mound builders, well known for their earth works in Ohio and West Virginia. This name (Adena) is relatively modern: the name actually comes from excavations on an estate owned by Thomas Worthington (1773-1827), the sixth governor of Ohio. Adena may have been a fine name for Governor Worthington's farm, but it is an anathema to modern-day ancestors of the Native Americans in Ohio. They maintain that the Native American oral traditions have preserved the correct name for the Adena: they were the Azgens, otherwise known as the Moon-Eyed People. Mounds were used for burial structures, ceremonial sites, historical markers, and perhaps even as gathering places. They vary from as little as 20 feet to as much as 300 feet in diameter and considering the effort it would have taken to construct them, the mounds very clearly had significance to the Native Americans.

The Monongahela who came after them faded away for reasons still unclear to modern scholars: perhaps their maize-based agriculture failed during the Little Ice Age (13th through 19th centuries) as some believe. Perhaps they fell victim to two successive periods of drought (1587-1589 and 1607-1612), or they became exposed to diseases spread by other Native Americans engaged in trade with the white man. They may have been killed off or assimilated by other more powerful tribes such as the Iroquois or Lenape. Regardless of the cause, by the 1630s they had disappeared from the southwestern Pennsylvania landscape.

Evidence of the presence of mounds and numerous Native American villages has been documented throughout Greene County as early as the turn of the 20th century. Noted local historian and Waynesburg College Professor Andrew Jackson Waychoff (1849-1927) made references to a mound in Franklin Township three miles south of Waynesburg in his book *History of Greene County Pennsylvania*. A collector of local artifacts, Professor Waychoff was instrumental in the creation of the Greene County Historical Society during the 1920s. Documentation of villages at the Lapping and nearby Gordon farms exists but downplay some intriguing details.

Contemporary newspaper articles mention that the Lapping family accidentally disturbed a series of small graves on the same farm; at the time, no one had any idea of the long-term consequences that would unfold from this.

According to the newspaper report, Professor Waychoff and others were called to investigate a group of unusual graves discovered by the Lappings as they plowed ground in preparation for planting corn. The graves were in a circle encompassing roughly an acre and spaced at 50-foot intervals. Each grave opened contained the remains of diminutive mature adults. Their remains were folded with knees near chins, interred in shallow graves reported to be two feet by one-and-a-half feet by nine inches in depth.

Not all the graves were opened, but those that were had a flat stone cover of three feet. Remains that were examined had been buried with a variety of artifacts: necklaces of animal teeth, large fish bones and polished bone; flint darts, tools, pottery and at least one piece of copper that possibly could have been an early gorget. In old Europe a gorget was a cloth worn around the neck. Eventually the gorgets became part of military uniforms, made of metal such as those worn by the Nazis.

The tallest of the individuals exhumed would have been three to four feet in height. A local named Chauncey Sayers took photographs of both the graves and their occupants. Professor Waychoff contacted the Smithsonian Institution for information regarding the discoveries. For a time, locals could see some of the skeletons and relics at Morris & Sayers, a Waynesburg business. What Waychoff learned from the Smithsonian, if anything, has been lost to history or even suppressed.

The Little People

Remains of small-statured humans have also been found in other locations throughout the US, not only in the west but also in Ohio and Tennessee. *Harper's Magazine* in 1869 followed up on reports from Tennessee newspapers that described similar discoveries of "very little people... in tombs of stone."

In her book *The Lost History of the Little People,* author Susan Martinez, PhD, recalls tales of diminutive humans, the Little People, from all over the world. Folklore from around the world describe different kinds of Little People; some were helpful to humans and others not. North America is no exception: Native American tradition speaks of Little People on this continent. Little People turn up in South America, Hawaii, Sumatra, and even Java; however, the "hobbit" of Java was discovered 200 years after graves of small individuals were found all over the United States.

29

Based on discovered burial grounds and other evidence from around the world Martinez suggests that the Little People were not legend, but flesh and blood. Could it be possible that what was unearthed at the Lapping farm were remains of a little understood, or perhaps little publicized race of small Native Americans?

The Moon-Eyed People

The Moon-Eyed People are literally the stuff of legend. Appearing in the traditions and oral histories of several Native American nations, they also appear in the written history of white settlers. The Azgen were the earliest of the mound builders; in fact, according to Native American oral tradition they were the first here, period. They are said to have been small in stature, pale or white-skinned, blue-eyed with blond hair, and nocturnal in nature to the point of avoiding light (thus the Moon-Eyed moniker).

The Azgen were sky watchers and tracked time by watching the night sky. They lived in caves, underground, or in small round structures made of earth and wood. They cremated their dead but buried their shamans intact. Their homeland is said to have encompassed much of Appalachia: Greene County, host to the Adena, was in fact home to the Azgen.

Some literature describes the Azgen as a peaceful people while other sources state they so aggressively defended their homes that other Native Americans gave them a wide berth. They have been portrayed by whites as blood-drinking night fighters or having come from Atlantis. Regardless of who or what they were, they seem to have been here prior to the tribes and Indian nations more familiar to white culture.

Assuming that Waychoff would not lend his reputation to fraud or hoaxing, then it is entirely possible that a unique burial ground was uncovered on at least one farm in Greene County. At the very least the Lapping farm, and possibly one or two adjacent properties played host to the destruction of Native American burials. While the Lapping find took place after local skirmishes between whites and Indians had ceased, it nevertheless involved disturbance of a fairly large burial ground. As a consequence, strange phenomena have occurred in the area up to present times.

It is unclear whether the Moon-Eyed People were capable of harnessing supernatural power. Some have speculated that they were merely of this world but were not to be trifled with. They were dangerous to encounter at night and had a reputation for ferocity – they reputedly drank the blood of their victims in order to maintain their strength while hunting. Some researchers suggest that the Moon-Eyed People were remembered as a distinct group of humans who were physically very different from Native Americans.

Lewis and Clark camped on a hill near the Teton River in 1804 that was a manmade mound that local Dakota referred to as the "Mountain of the Little People" or the "Spirit Mound." According to Dakota elders the original inhabitants were enlightened and extremely spiritual. The Cherokee word *adawehi* is associated with shamans and at times Moon-Eyed People; it describes not only the shaman himself but all that is divine and surrounds the invisible world that permeates and empowers the living. The term also applies to the shaman's familiar spirits that can be invoked for assistance. Those well versed in *adawehi* could not only shapeshift but become invisible as well. It is entirely possible that the Moon-Eyed people were as adept at harnessing and applying the powers of the natural world as they were at nocturnal fighting and hunting. Regardless, they were dreaded as enemies and frequently it took considerable effort to displace them.

Disturbing the unknown

Historical accounts of the county state that scores of Native American villages that once dotted our landscape are now lost to history. Unwitting present-day residents run the risk of disturbing the hidden past, revealing previously unknown Native American sites.

The home of the Hunter family (not their real name) sits atop unusual, mound-like topography. When their foundation required excavation work, a surprising discovery was made. As the contractor removed the ground from around the house he discovered traces of what appeared to be Native American pottery and human remains. When shown the artifacts, the Hunters realized that the items should not be discarded along with other construction debris. They instructed the contractor to gather everything that had been discovered and set it aside for safekeeping. The work crew was incredulous but complied with their request.

Shortly after the discovery, the family began noticing a foul odor in the house, but only at night. During the daylight hours and even into the early evening, there was no noticeable smell. However, each night, regardless of atmospheric conditions, a very strong and distinct smell similar to rotting roadkill would enter their dwelling around 10 PM. No amount of air freshener, candles or window fans could dissipate it. Once their foundation work was completed, they instructed their contractor to replace the artifacts to their approximate location and cover them once again with earth. The nightly odor vanished and did not return.

A similar case occurred in Center Township, just west of Waynesburg. The Brown family (not their real name) was excited to break ground to construct a new house to replace one they had outgrown. The contractor they hired to do foundation work began excavating near the crest of a hill only to uncover an apparent Indian burial site. The remains were reinterred, and construction continued without incident. Their new home was completed and occupied soon after.

The following year the family noticed their dog would often sit outside late in the afternoon and stare at the same area, sometimes several times a week. Soon after, they began to hear laughter of a child at play, seemingly a young girl, coming from the same area that so often held their dog's attention. On one occasion some jewelry belonging to their youngest daughter went missing, only to be discovered some time later on the fireplace mantle. None of the members of the Brown family had taken the jewelry or placed it there.

Mrs. Brown has heard the laughter several times and has also heard a child's voice saying hello. However, to date the majority of activity has been the laughter of one or more unseen children who seem to be content in letting the family know he/she finds something to be amusing or perhaps they are happy to have some company. The paranormal activity has been confined to prankish behavior, chiefly the relocation of objects, and the sounds of a little girl's voice.

The Native American presence, while well documented by historians, contains gaps that quite often miss the location of numerous Native American villages or gathering places. The Brown family's home is one such location. While experts may assume it was an area where contact with Native Americans was very likely there is no official documented evidence. Further, in this case it cannot be assumed that the Brown family's giggling visitor is Native American. The Brown family to date seems to be visited by a well-meaning spirit from the past. However, not all ephemeral visitations are benign and if Native American in origin, the visitation could be shamanistic in nature.

The psychic imprint of shamans

There is evidence that Greene County was once a focal point for the passing on of shamanistic practices and traditions. Given the number of intact graves and the artifacts discovered on the Lapping farm it is possible that rituals were practiced there by shamans. The jaws of mountain lions have been found in Azgen (Adena) graves elsewhere. By wearing the bones of animals, shamans took on the characteristics of the animals themselves.

In addition, use of animal bones ritualistically or as jewelry may have assisted in shapeshifting by shamans into other forms. Shapeshifting is a soul journey that taps into the powers and information available in the natural world. Shamans made these journeys on behalf of their communities or to gain power and information for themselves to be used in helping others.

While this may be an over simplification of the historic role of shamans, it does give us a sense of the responsibility they carried in regard to their communities, ancestors and descendants. They influenced political power as well. We can certainly visualize them calling upon their skills and powers to try to stop the inevitable destruction and desecration of their ancestral homelands by the invading, interloping and untrustworthy men with white skin.

In comparison, did not the white men call upon their entire arsenal – physical, spiritual and technological – in their quest to drive out the people with red skin? When faced with military, political and societal destruction, leaders will fight with whatever weapons they have at hand. Perhaps some of the paranormal activity today is a remnant of the manifestation of spiritual powers deployed long ago by shamans. The military and political battles were lost long ago, but spiritually the fight may be continuing today, carried on by apparitions, grave guardians, mysterious entities and unseen laughing children.

The Freeport mound site

Of the well-known Greene County Native American archaeological sites, most are attributed to the Monongahela, with one associated with the Azgen (Adena): the Freeport Site. The Freeport Site is markedly different from the others and may have been another shamanic power center.

Encompassing some 11 acres, the Freeport site, as its name implies, is located somewhere within Freeport Township in western Greene County. It was first recorded in the 1950s and for at least nine years was studied by university field teams. More recently, a well-known and respected consulting firm from the Pittsburgh area conducted an exhaustive study of the site funded by Alpha Natural Resources. Consultants expecting to complete the excavation of a small Azgen (Adena) mound and village were surprised to discover an extensive field of artifacts from a site occupied intermittently for over 2,000 years, with the most intensive occupation taking place 600 years ago.

Experts did not discover the typical small village encompassing the mound on site; rather, they discovered crescent-shaped clusters of features and patterns for structures never seen in southwestern Pennsylvania. In addition, the artifacts discovered were not typical for this area, as many were ceremonial. Few arrow points, which would indicate hunting and food preparation, were uncovered.

As the mound excavation progressed, 31 features were discovered and over 3000 artifacts were revealed. The mound had been significantly

34

enlarged, and a Sacred Circle had been built centuries later that surrounded it. Further exploration below the plow line brought to light extensive earthworks, the construction of which would have required knowledge of astronomy, design and planning. Creation of these earthworks would have been a major undertaking.

The village did not contain evidence of round wigwams typical of western Pennsylvania. Instead a large rectangular building, sweat houses, fences, screens and other unique buildings were documented. In total, the Freeport site contained 448 mapped archaeological features, as well was as human burials, caches, earth ovens, hearths, pot holders, an intentional puppy burial, a possible buried drum, evidence of pottery production and nut processing, and what appeared to have been a tattoo parlor. As work continued, researchers became convinced that the Freeport site clearly involved rituals and had been used by a prehistoric society for healing and training of both male and female shamans.

Recovered from the site were human remains, 31,000 artifacts, 34,000 botanical remains, incised ceramics, stone tools, arrow points, stone tablets and carved stones. It is the largest assemblage of bone tools, decorative elements, gaming pieces and bone artifacts to have been uncovered in this part of Pennsylvania. It certainly seems that what we now know as the Freeport site was an area of great interest and importance to the Native Americans.

While Native American artifacts and traces of their circles, villages and burials are often found in low lying areas near water sources or streams, there have been discoveries made on the hilltops as well. When springtime plowing of crop fields was much more prevalent here, it was not unusual for farmers to find arrowheads and other artifacts in their cornfields. The decline of conventional tillage in favor of no-till agricultural practices, combined with an overall decline in row crop production in Greene County, may have significantly reduced the number of artifacts discovered. This in no way means there are no more sites of archaeological or spiritual significance to discover, but rather their discovery may be harder in the absence of archaeological research, earth disturbances by modern machinery, or admission and tracking of strange, unexplained sightings and events.

35

The fate of the mounds

Except for known archaeological sites and unknown mounds accidentally discovered, the locations and fate of untold numbers of mounds remains uncertain.

Experts point to proof that successive populations utilized sites as evidenced by the archaeological record. In contrast to the whites, it seems that later populations of Native Americans recognized the work of their predecessors, augmenting rather than destroying it. Case in point would be the work of the mound builders at the Freeport site who added a Sacred Circle and enlarged the existing mound centuries after the original construction. Clearly the Freeport site was important to succeeding generations of Native Americans. It may have influenced the construction of the Crow's Mills mounds and possibly others. Defending them against destruction by whites may have spurred long gone warriors to commit atrocities in a failed attempt to dislodge whites and discourage further westward expansion.

Neglect, lack of interest and continuing development have literally buried many mounds. Their artifacts remain, however, along with the energy and power attached to them. Who knows how many may yet be discovered – and release their ancient residues in haunting ways?

CHAPTER 4

STRANGE ACTIVITY NEAR LAPPING FARM

The area around the Lapping farm in Franklin Township, with its Native American burial mound and disturbed graves, has been the site of ongoing paranormal activity, including ghosts, mystery cats, and two strange "inhumanoids" known as Lizard Man and Frog Man.

Lizard Man

According to local newspaper reports, in the 1890s two men were hunting in Franklin Township when they encountered what they described as a "Lizard Man." The creature was described in what today's terminology could be considered a reptilian: essentially a humanoid reptile walking on two legs. According to a newspaper account, the men were struck with fear and the Lizard Man seized one of the men. Evidently the creature was quite strong but slow moving. Tucking his hapless victim under one arm, it began slowly shuffling away. The second hunter ran for help, and

Lizard Man carts off a hunter. Credit: John Weaver.

upon returning to the site with a number of other men began tracking Lizard Man through the brush. The men eventually caught up with the Reptilian as it approached a large hole in the ground. Upon seeing the other men approaching, Lizard Man dropped his prize, went down the hole and vanished from sight. The two hunters, joined by the other men, then piled rocks and debris into the opening until it was sealed. Allegedly, Lizard Man was never seen again – at least for some time.

Lizard Man sightings have been reported elsewhere for more than a century, and into modern times. Some of the most famous are in Kentucky, where amphibious-looking, gilled and web-footed lizard-humanoids have been spotted near the Ohio River. One case occurred in 1966, documented by Barton M. Nunnelly in *Mysterious Kentucky Vol. 1* (2007; 2017). The Lizard Man, estimated at five-foot six inches to six feet tall, was seen where Sinking Creek meets the Ohio. Sinking Creek is believed to connect to a huge underwater system that connects caverns in Western Kentucky – an interesting similarity to the Franklin Township case in which Lizard Man went down a hole.

Mystery cats

Fast forward now to the 1960s and 1970s, when Lizard Man – or some shapeshifted form of it – was seen again. In fact, the area was rife with other paranormal activity. There were sightings of large cats in the area. One was reported to be very similar to a black panther and had been seen skulking around a residential neighborhood at night. Later, others reported seeing what appeared to be a mountain lion in the area during daylight hours.

For a number of years, the large cats seemed to have vanished, only to return in the past few years. In Pennsylvania, mountain lions are officially extinct, yet sightings continue to this day. In 2016 there were two sightings in the same residential neighborhood where the black panther had been seen, again at dusk or after dark. Another individual – I'll call him Robert – got a good look at a very large cat crossing a road adjacent to the Lapping farm in broad daylight. He reported that it did indeed look like a mountain lion, right down to the tip of the tail. Robert was able to make a good judgment of the cat's size in comparison to the guard rails and fence posts along the roadway and the cat was far too big to be a common house cat or even a bobcat.

Perhaps what Robert and the other eyewitnesses saw were actual flesh-and-blood mountain lions in present-day Franklin Township. Perhaps not. Could they have seen imprints of long-ago shapeshifting shamans still acting in their community's interest by taking the form of a large cat? Whether or not shamans were present at the Lapping farm site can be debated, but shamans were here in Greene County prior to the arrival of the white man and are represented in the archaeological record.

House with a ghostly bonus

From 1967 to 1975, a newlywed couple I'll call Kurt and Vicky moved into a house that was literally a stone's throw from both the Lapping farm as well as where Robert reported sighting a mountain lion. As newlyweds, they were thrilled to find a partially furnished house with affordable rent. The home had been built by a well-known Waynesburg family to be used as a summer home many years prior. It was perched on the same ridge that ran through the Lapping farm and was well situated to take full advantage of not only natural light but also any available summer breeze.

The house was well built and somewhat of a time capsule, for some of the furnishings were old but in good repair. Only one piece of furniture, a classic Victorian-style couch, was removed by the landlord after Kurt and Vicky moved in. The attic was spacious and a considerable number of old but well-preserved toys were stored there as well.

Gradually Kurt and Vicky began to realize they were not alone in the house. Both began to see a wispy outline of a woman in the living room in the same general location. She usually appeared after dark but didn't seem to be aware of Kurt and Vicky's presence. There was nothing malevolent about the apparition, and the couple never feared her presence. She seemed to be attached to a particular piece of furniture in the living room for she was always seen near it.

Other phenomena reinforced the impression that the residence was haunted. The house was constructed before the advent of air conditioning and the couple relied on natural ventilation and supplemental fans for cooling in the summer. However, Vicky noticed that some rooms even on the hottest days of summer remained cold, so much so that when the door was closed a draft of cold air coming under the door was always present. Voices could be heard in rooms where no one was present, and footsteps could be heard going up and down the stairs as well as moving about on the upper floor.

One startling sighting occurred when a cousin of Vicky's, whom I'll call Dan, was visiting from Ohio. During his visit, on one occasion Dan returned to his bedroom to retrieve something from the closet. Upon opening the door, Dan came face to face with the apparition of a young boy. Dan was startled, and the boy vanished. Upon telling Kurt and Vicky of his encounter, Dan learned that neither had seen the lad.

After Dan went home, Vicky asked the caretaker who lived next door if he had any idea who the young man may have been. The caretaker told Vicky that the boy was probably the younger brother of their landlord who had been struck by a car and died from his injuries when he was nine years of age. He also added that the young man had died on the Victorian couch that was removed shortly after Kurt and Vicky's arrival as tenants.

Intrigued by this story, and having known the caretaker, I researched Kurt and Vicky's landlord and she did have a younger brother who died at age nine. Regrettably the caretaker did not provide any insight as to the identity of the other apparition. Despite their proximity to the Lapping farm, neither Kurt nor Vicky ever noticed anything unusual outside of their home. At no time did they feel threatened or fearful.

Their daughter, Heather, had experiences as well. She too saw the wispy white apparition of a woman, but she always lacked detail. Like cousin Dan, she saw the boy but more often. When opening her wardrobe at times he would be there, just as Dan had seen him. He never seemed to notice Heather and was dressed in clothing similar to that

41

worn in the early 1900s. Sometimes he would seem to be playing, and at other times inactive. Like Dan, she thought the boy to be eight to nine years of age.

The Frog Man

One afternoon in the early spring of 1973, Heather's father, Kurt, was fishing in the pond located on the farm property. A path connected the pond to both the caretaker's house and the house where Kurt, Vicky and Heather lived. Heather started down the path to go see her father as he fished. While the majority of the path was open, a very small portion cut through a wooded area in a depression. This area was the only part of the path not seen from either house. Both Heather and Vicky had thought that particular spot to be foreboding, as it left them with the impression they were being watched.

After spending some time with her father at the pond, Heather took the path homeward. Upon reaching the wooded area she suddenly felt that something was out of place. Looking up, she saw what she thought at first was a giant bullfrog sitting on a fallen log.

But this was no bullfrog. What she saw was a slender, humanoid figure, four to five feet in height and with large, shiny silver eyes. The creature, although humanoid, appeared to be reptilian in nature but had frog-like features on its head. It had no hair, no clothes, and its smooth skin was a sickly gray color. There were no ears or nose. Heather froze for a moment and was about 10 feet from the creature. It stared at her with its silvery eyes, bared its teeth, and began hissing at her.

Terrified, Heather ran back to her father. The creature was not seen again.

Despite all the paranormal goings on, this was the only time Heather felt threatened while living there.

There are other reports of frog-like men in the US. The most famous is the Loveland Frogmen of Loveland, Ohio, just outside of

Cincinnati to the northeast. In March of 1955, a witness reported seeing three "frog-like" men along a road just outside Loveland. An unidentified businessman saw three unusual creatures one May evening standing alongside a road not far from the Little Miami River. Stopping his car, he claimed to have observed them for three to five minutes. They were three to four feet tall and covered with leathery skin. They stood erect, were bipedal, and had the heads and faces of frogs. They appeared to be hairless, had webbed hands and feet, and deep wrinkles on their heads. The businessman also reported that one of the creatures held a metallic-looking device that resembled a wand. The creature held the object over its head and it emitted a series of flashes of light. Becoming even more fearful, the businessman fled the area.

Lack of more specific details on this report have spurred discussion over the years as to its authenticity, but the Loveland Frogman would return.

On March 3, 1972 at about 1 AM, a police officer witnessed an identical creature in the same general area along the Little Miami River. The policeman reported that he was driving slowly, due to the substantial amount of ice on the road, when he saw what looked like a dog sitting by the curb.

Suddenly, the animal darted in front of the cruiser, forcing the officer to slam on the brakes in order to avoid a potential collision. Once the cruiser came to a sudden halt, the headlights fully illuminated the creature. The officer is quoted as saying, "In the span of seconds this crouching, frog-like creature stood up on its two back legs, which were much longer than its front two. It turned and stared back at my vehicle, then quickly scrambled over the guardrail and hurried down the embankment, finally disappearing into the Little Miami River."

Descriptions of the first witness and the police officer, while 17 years apart, are similar: the police officer described the creature as being three to four feet tall and possibly weighing in the area of 50 to 75 pounds. He also stated that its skin had a leathery texture and that the animal's features resembled those of an overgrown frog mixed with the body of a man.

Another officer investigated the scene later that evening. He saw no sign of the creature but reported that there were definite and distinct "scratch" marks on the guardrail where the animal purportedly crossed as well as a few deep tracks leading down the embankment.

Two weeks later another officer, Mark Mathews, was in the same area at night and driving slowly due to icy road conditions. Officer Mathews spotted what he thought was a dead dog or coyote in the road. Given driving conditions, a dead animal in the road was a significant hazard, and Mathews stopped to drag the carcass to the side of the road.

Upon exiting his cruiser, he was startled when the "carcass" sat up in a crouching position. Drawing his weapon, Mathews fired at it and it scurried over the guardrail toward the Little Miami River. Both officers contributed to a composite sketch of the creature that featured its stocky build as well as webbed fingers and toes.

Later in the same year a local farmer was checking his fields when he spotted four frog-like "men." They too had "frog heads" with large eyes. Unlike the other Loveland Frogmen sightings, these four were reported to have wide mouths and teeth. Their skin was described as being greenish-gray in color. Just as in the other sightings, the Frog Men made their escape by scurrying toward the Little Miami River.

In August 2016 a young man named Sam Jacobs was playing Pokémon GO with his girlfriend in the same general area of the first three sightings. They saw a giant frog-like creature sitting near the water that clearly was not part of their game. Much to their surprise, the giant "frog" stood on its hind legs and began to walk. Jacobs was able to obtain both photographs and video of the creature. All were unrevealing except to show a bright pair of shining eyes. Jacobs contacted a local newspaper, which covered the story briefly until Officer Mathews went public in a seeming attempt to debunk his own story of the Loveland Frogman.

Mathews not only contradicted the original version of the encounter, he also revealed the identity of the first officer who encountered the creature to be Ray Shockey. Mathews claimed what actually happened was that he shot and killed an animal three to three-and-a-half feet in height, scooped it up off the road, and placed it in the trunk of his cruiser. He said he showed it to fellow officer Shockey who confirmed it was the same creature he had seen. Mathews then claimed the creature was identified as a very large, tailless, sickly iguana that was either released by its owner or had escaped. He also stated he had told this very same story to an author writing a book on urban legends but when it went to print no mention was made of the creature's true identity. Mathews said he believes the animal survived cold Ohio winters by living around warm water discharge pipes of a nearby factory.

Was the Loveland Frogman in fact a very large, ill iguana? The probability of one very large iguana surviving the Loveland winters (average temperature 44 degrees) becomes even more incredulous when stretched to include others in the same area. Even while allegedly basking in the factory-warmed waters, it is hard to picture a cold-blooded iguana moving about in weather cold enough for road surfaces to freeze as Mathews originally reported, let alone find something to eat.

In 2016 Mathews stated he was tired of talking about the Frogman, and that the Jacobs sighting was a hoax. Perhaps, but why wait 44 years to come clean and why identify a former co-worker and fellow law enforcement officer who at the time of the sightings did not wish to be identified? Mathews had contributed to the description leading to the sketch of the Frogman – why the sudden change of heart?

While the differences between Heather's encounter and the Loveland sightings are apparent, it is important to note that they were in the same time frame (1972-1973), in springtime, and near water. In Heather's case it was a farm pond as opposed to the Little Miami River. Perhaps the most significant similarity is both the Ohio farmer and Heather reported seeing a wide mouth with teeth. While the little boy and wispy woman frequently seen could be attributed to a residual haunting, Heather's encounter with the creature on the log is something different. Is it possible that the Lizard Man reported in the newspaper had been seen again? Was it the same type of creature as the Loveland Frogman? An even bigger question to ponder: Were these creatures denizens of some netherworld next to our reality – or are they remnants of some long-ago shapeshifting shamanic activity by the Azgen on the nearby Lapping farm?

Chapter 5

Black Blobs and Mole Things

Are there spirits or entities that guard the sites of Native American mounds, artifacts and burials? Greene County residents have had some terrifying encounters with shapeshifting entities that do not appreciate disturbances of the landscape.

The "things" start out as black blobs of various sizes that seem to flow along just above the ground. They change shape and size to travel through wooded areas and into buildings. They move astonishingly fast.

According to witnesses, the black blobs occasionally attack people who are sleeping outdoors, most often from behind or from the side, in the shapeshifted form of a "mole thing," a creature resembling a mole with exceptionally sharp clawed feet. Curiously, those who have encountered these things have worked at locations either at or near where Native American artifacts have been found. Some victims have made their homes adjacent to or on top of Native American burial sites.

A man I know named John (who does not want his full name revealed), a local handyman, began experiencing encounters with the blob/mole things shortly after finding a stone mortar, such as that used with a pestle, under a porch while remodeling a residence in Wayne Township that dated to the late 18th century. Upon finding the artifact, it was compared to others that were known to be of Native American origin and found to be very similar.

As work progressed, he began encountering black blobs frequently on his way to the job site. Often, they would be seen drifting across the road or darting behind trees as he worked. Soon he began seeing them at home as well, in both black blob and mole thing forms. Frequently in the night, he would have nightmares where scurrying mole things used their clawed feet to climb up his sheets into his bed and would attempt to cut holes in his back as he slept. In one particularly fearful dream, a black blob came into his bedroom by flowing under the door and up over the foot of the bed in an apparent attempt to suffocate him. Jolted out of sleep by fear, he was astonished to see a large, black blob lying on top of his sheets.

A black blob "mole thing" attacks a sleeping man. Credit: John Weaver.

According to other members of his family, he had gone to bed early and was in the bedroom alone when they began hearing unintelligible shouts and frantic activity. Bursting into the room, they found him literally fighting something only he could see. Once the door opened, the blob burst into several small pieces and disappeared into the walls and floor. John's wife and children, however, saw nothing.

On another occasion, again having turned in early and sleeping alone, he was attacked by a creature that manifested as a black entity with large armadillo-like feet that sped along the wall, dropped into the bed by his side and began cutting a hole in his back. Once again, the other members of the family heard shouts and a commotion coming from the bedroom. Upon entering, they saw the fully awake man holding something that could not be seen and beating it with his fist. As the work progressed, John returned the mortar to where he had discovered it, covering it with the new porch floor. Since that time the encounters with attacking things have nearly ceased.

Another family who asked to remain anonymous has had encounters with similar entities as well. For a number of years, they lived in a rented house in a rural part of Whiteley Township that was plagued by visits from mole things. Rather than attack the family aggressively, the scurrying entities seemed content to merely make their presence known.

The entities associated themselves with the family dog, a beagle, and would come and go through the front door quite often when the beagle was let in or out of the house. Frequently, when family members were reading or watching television, a mole thing would come into the room and sit beside them as if mimicking their dog. Engrossed in whatever they were focused upon at the time, family members would not realize it was a horrific creature until the beagle entered the room and the entity would vanish.

While no one in the household had ever discovered Native American artifacts in or around their home, their next-door neighbor had. Several years before they rented the house, a construction project was initiated on the adjoining property a few hundred yards away, which required earth moving. Once digging began, the landowner realized he had disturbed an unknown Native American burial site: human remains, pottery fragments, and other artifacts were discovered. The remains and artifacts were replaced in the ground, and the construction site was moved in order to proceed without further disturbance. Work was completed a few yards away without any additional discoveries.

Perhaps this explains the appearance of the mole things and their more prankster-like approach to the tenants of the rental property, who relocated and had no more encounters with the entities.

CHAPTER 6

FREAKY FRANKLIN TOWNSHIP

Centered on the map of Greene County is Franklin Township, which bustles with economic activity. It is home to the majority of the county's shops, restaurants and motels as well as the fairgrounds and airport. It also has the dubious honor of hosting all the county's prisoners both local and state. It surrounds the county seat of Waynesburg.

Franklin Township over the years has seen its share of hardship, as evidenced by the brutal 1999 murder of Ira Swearingen, an apparent hate crime. Mr. Swearingen was shot in the head one cold dark night for committing the crime of being in the wrong place at the wrong time. Sadly, this is just one more name added to the litany of those unfortunate souls who precede him. Like the rest of the county, many are the victims whose blood was violently shed in Franklin Township up to and after its creation in 1787.

About the same time, in the late 1700s, three brothers, Simon, Thomas and John Rinehart, arrived from Germany and claimed by priority of right the area of the Coal Lick Creek watershed in Franklin Township. They lived on the fringes of Fort Jackson, located in what is now Waynesburg, and themselves were victims of attacks by Native Americans. When alarmed, the Rineharts retreated to the safer confines of Fort Jackson in what is now Waynesburg to escape Indian raiding parties.

On one such occasion at least one of the Rineharts disappeared while attempting to tend to his cattle. His body was never found; all that attested to his departure was some of his hair and blood on the ground near the cattle pen. His survivors concluded at the time that his body must have been cut to pieces and scattered to hide the evidence. Simon Rinehart was also killed in the spring of 1779 by Native Americans.

The Rineharts played an important role in the early years of Greene County, and played an expected and perhaps unwelcome role in establishing the homestead that became known as the county poor farm, which is now home to the Greene County Historical Society. As previously mentioned, the Rineharts once dominated the Coal Lick Creek watershed, and I was lucky enough to have spent much of my youth there. The Rineharts represent some of my ancestors, and from time to time I heard tales from the verbal history of my predecessors.

One such tale was of the Indian Rock, a large piece of what appeared to be sandstone perched on a ridge top along a long-gone stretch of Dark Hollow Road not far from the present location of the local radio station tower. According to verbal accounts, the Indian Rock was some sort of gathering point where the local Indians would dance. While I have seen the Indian Rock, it is long gone, having been quite unceremoniously removed during the construction of I-79 in the 1960s. While its original resting place was obliterated along with the darkest part of Dark Hollow Road, anecdotal information indicates some effort was made to relocate the Indian Rock, but it did not withstand the stress and broke into pieces.

Whether or not it was an actual gathering place for Native Americans will likely never be known but given the close proximity of the Rineharts and the Indians, it may be possible that there was some validity to the stories. In addition, research for this book has confirmed that there was a strong Native American presence in the vicinity of the Indian Rock and corroborates the verbal history of the Coal Lick watershed as it relates to locations of Indian activity.

Interestingly, the site of the former Indian Rock is within walking distance of where Ira Swearingen met his fate overlooking the valley claimed by the Rineharts and contested by the Indians.

Historical Society ghosts

Scarcely a mile from Indian Rock stands the Rinehart homestead that later became the Greene County poor farm and current home to the Greene County Historical Society. The county poor farm gained some notoriety for its harsh treatment of inmates following an exposé published in 1886 by the *Atlantic Monthly* that drew public attention to the plight of poor farm inmates all over the country. The county poor farm continued until the late 1960s when the building, then in disrepair, was abandoned for a more modern facility across the road.

While the poor farm residents are long gone, the stigma associated with their treatment remains. Where once the indigent, the mentally challenged and the abandoned lived, worked and ate, one now finds the displays, artifacts and collections of the historical society. Where people and horses once toiled to raise crops to feed the poor farm population, one now finds students, families and visitors walking leisurely over the grounds and through the 52 rooms of the building. The Greene County Historical Society finds itself in the very shadows of the Rineharts and their bloody skirmishes with Native Americans, the departed Indian Rock, and the collective lives and unmarked graves of the poor farm residents.

Is it any wonder that the Historical Society is haunted?

For years there have been reports of shadowy figures and strange encounters almost from day one when the Historical Society moved in to the Rinehart homestead. One former board member reported hearing loud moans coming from the basement: a *mmmmmmm* sound. It was assumed to be caused by a bird or other wildlife, but a quick investigation revealed nothing. Later this same person encountered people in 19th-century attire in one of the museum's many rooms at a time when no visitors were scheduled.

Staff members hear voices where there should be none, interns encounter unexpected figures passing by, and a red-haired boy has been seen in the barn. A figure in green fatigues was seen by a former administrator in the museum's library, and the same person also heard men's voices and what sounded like boxes being moved when no one else was present. Lights blink on and off by themselves, ghostly images are captured in photographs, and objects are found out of place with no apparent explanation.

The Historical Society, for better or worse, has promoted its paranormal activity by sponsoring paid ghost hunts and Flashlight Fright Nights as fundraisers for the organization. The jury is still out, paranormally speaking, as to whether there will be any unexpected encounters or unexplained events caused by these efforts. While it no doubt takes a considerable amount of funding to operate and maintain the building, is the Historical Society tempting the proverbial hand of fate by doing so? What is it that haunts the building: ghosts of previous owners, former poor home residents, demons, land spirits, Native Americans, or a little of each?

Mystery big cats

Upstream from the Greene County Historical Society and still in the shadow of the Indian Rock are the headwaters of Coal Lick Creek. As time and generations passed so did the ownership of the farmland of Coal Lick Creek. I spent many years hearing tales of that valley. Among other things I heard tales of men hanging themselves out of despair, packs of wild dogs wreaking havoc at night and mountain lions in the Coal Lick watershed.

A trusted and now deceased family member told me of days of her youth when it was common to hear the scream of big cats, particularly at dusk. Those of us who have heard the howl of bobcats will attest that it is something once heard and never forgotten. The screams described to me were not that of a bobcat, however, but of a mountain lion. It would sit near the top of a hill overlooking a farmhouse and would "holler at the setting sun."

Described as being so blood curdling as to make hair stand literally on end, this particular cat drew the attention of neighbors until it was shot and killed in the late 1940s. I knew the man who helped the mountain lion enter the afterlife, and he is also deceased. However, the family member who told me the story was not prone to telling tall tales and I believed the account as told to me when I was a youth. It is interesting to note that Barnet Rinehart's former homestead which is located within the same valley was first known as "Lion Bush."

The Pennsylvania Game Commission will tell you that the last mountain lion was killed in Pennsylvania in 1896, and that current reports are simply misidentified domestic cats or escaped exotic pets. Personal experience contradicts that, for in 1969 I witnessed a mountain lion in Franklin Township directly across from my parents' home, within walking distance of both the Indian Rock and the present day historical society.

It was traveling through a meadow on a summer day in a leisurely fashion, its long tail trailing. This was no misidentification of a house cat as I got a good look at it when it slowed at a woven wire fence. Contrasted by the fence post and woven wire, the cat was easily over two feet tall and effortlessly cleared the barbed wire that topped the fence. The only other witness was our family dog who attempted to give chase but was easily outdistanced by the cat. It clearly had the appearance and stature of a mountain lion.

My parents were highly skeptical of my sighting. In recent years, however, I have gathered credible reports of similar sightings very close to where I had my encounter. Two sightings were described to me, one in a populated area of Franklin Township and another along Route 19 at Gordon Hill in 2013-14. I have also seen pictures of mountain lions captured by game cameras from other areas of Greene County in the recent past. The big cats are here and have been in the past.

Why don't wildlife officials want to admit it?

CHAPTER 7

SPECTRAL RESIDENTS OF WAYNESBURG

Waynesburg was founded in 1796 and serves as the county seat. It is surrounded on all sides by Franklin Township. The town has been the scourge of many a youth lamenting the fact that there is nothing to do in Waynesburg. To be sure, entertainment opportunities for both the young and the restless could be described as few and far between. Perhaps they just need to look between the cracks into the realm of the unseen.

Waynesburg hosts a business district, although it is but a shadow of its former self, thanks to big box retailers and the internet. My father was well acquainted with the trials and tribulations associated with managing a small business in Waynesburg. He said often that Waynesburg (and Greene County) neither boomed nor went bust, but just plodded along. As a young lad I heartily agreed and thought if artist Norman Rockwell ever did paintings of Waynesburg he would accurately reflect daily life by merely hanging blank canvas. Such are the misconceptions of youth.

Restless Thomas Slater

Named after Revolutionary War hero General "Mad" Anthony Wayne, Waynesburg was once the home of Fort Jackson and was established on land owned by Thomas Slater, mentioned earlier as striving to establish peaceful relations with the Native Americans. Slater obtained the property from an unknown person or persons who had laid claim to the land via a "tomahawk improvement."

Tomahawk improvements were a method of land claim in which a person would walk the perimeter of an area they wished to claim and mark the boundary through a series of marks made in the bark of trees with a sharp tool or tomahawk. Many times, these boundaries were recognized as legitimate, and the claimed property could be resold to others, as was the case with Slater's purchase of his new home. He paid the princely sum of "one two-year-old heifer calf, one flint lock rifle, and some other trifling articles which the (other) fellow carried away with him."

Slater then set about constructing a cabin in which to live, and his 400-acre tract was eventually sold and became Waynesburg. No serious skirmishes with Native Americans took place within what is now the borough, but there were bloody exchanges very close by, such as the Brown massacre just east of town. While not nearly as spectacular in terms of sheer violence as other skirmishes with Native Americans, the Brown massacre is noteworthy for the method of escape by intended victim, Vincent Brown.

Vincent and his father, William, had stopped to chat with friends at a cemetery just east of Waynesburg when shots rang out. William and two other men fell dead and as the attacking Indians revealed themselves Vincent took flight with the warriors in hot pursuit. Young and athletic, Vincent proved difficult to overtake. He was soon faced with a difficult choice: stand, fight and most likely die; or leap off a 20-foot embankment into Ten Mile Creek. Without hesitation, Vincent chose the latter. He landed in Ten Mile, crossed to the other side, and escaped through the fields while his bewildered attackers looked on.

Over the years Waynesburg grew, eventually covering the entire tract. Some of the early influential residents lived, died and were buried in graves so poorly marked that they were lost to posterity. One such individual was attorney Robert Whitehill, who was described after his passing as "one of the profoundest lawyers, and brightest ornaments of the Waynesburg bar."

Many people were buried in a long-gone cemetery located "on the public common.... their graves were not marked and in time all recollection of the location of where they were interred was lost...." Tragic that the final resting places of individuals important to the establishment of a community could be lost, and their occupants were now beneath a sidewalk, a front porch, or in someone's crawlspace. Thus, much of the town is literally built upon the dead.

Not even Thomas Slater was able to find undisturbed rest in the afterlife. Upon his death in 1815, he was interred in the Methodist Church Cemetery (also known as the East End Cemetery or Hookstown Cemetery), which was once located between what are now Liberty and Porter Streets. By the early 1960s the cemetery was abandoned and following a court decision became the location of public housing. While a monument listing those known to be buried in the old Methodist Church Cemetery was erected in the nearby Greene Mount Cemetery, reports indicate that few or none of the remains were reinterred. As you may have guessed, the grave of Thomas Slater was one of the many that now plays host to housing.

But the story does not end there. In gathering information for this book, I was told a story of a woman who is reported to have visited certain offices in Waynesburg inquiring about Thomas Slater. At the time, this person resided in the housing development where the Methodist Church Cemetery once stood. Her interest reportedly was piqued by an apparition of a man that came out of her closet, claimed to be Thomas Slater and asked the startled tenant to learn as much as she could about him. Slater may be a bit restless in his grave.

That is an interesting tale, and one has to wonder about what effect building literally upon abandoned, unknown and unmarked graves could have on a community. Other reports mention strange activity on the north side of town around Burns Hall on the Waynesburg University campus and the adjoining cemetery.

Marker for Thomas Slater and the cemetery near Waynesburg University campus. Credit: Kevin Paul.

The university campus presents a challenge to ghost hunters and researchers. Locally and on the internet there are rumors of haunted buildings and ghostly encounters. Some staff members will confirm the rumors but not provide additional details. Our attempts to interview students, instructors, or university employees were fruitless. Those initially willing to share experiences became unavailable or unwilling to share their experiences even when promised absolute anonymity.

Beyond the campus, haunted houses and apartments all over town teem with phenomena such as shadow people, floating black entities and large spectral dogs.

Mr. Paintbrush and other specters

A huge spectral dog and other phenomena figure prominently in the experiences of the Linell family (not their real name) who have lived in Waynesburg for a number of years. Albert and Irene Linell are well educated and both work in professions that require observation skills and attention to detail. The Linells purchased a home that had been empty for a period of time but was exactly what they had been looking for: an older home of sound structure that had not been updated in recent memory.

The previous owners were Mr. and Mrs. John Preston (not their real names). Much of the original home interior remained and was in sound condition as it had been well cared for. Except for needing some cosmetic work, the house was capable of receiving its new owners and the Linells moved in immediately following purchase.

According to the older residents of the neighborhood the previous owners, the Prestons, had been financially successful but had a tumultuous marriage. John Preston was a well-known businessman while Carol Preston remained a stay-at-home mom. John was known as a skinflint while Carol, perhaps due to the stormy nature of their marriage, frequently consumed an excess of wine.

As Mr. and Mrs. Linell began work on their new home, they found there were a few items that needed repair: a downstairs door had a hole in it, the old window treatments simply had to go, and there was an odd blood-colored stain on one bedroom wall.

The drapes and shades were discarded immediately. The small hole in the door was not addressed and would figure in future occurrences. The blood-colored stain for weeks resisted every attempt to cover it. Following application of several coats of stain killer and paint it finally vanished from sight. That was a relief to Albert Linell, who had started to joke that perhaps they had purchased the proverbial house that dripped blood.

Joking aside, Albert did get uncomfortable in two areas of the house: the living room and one bedroom. At the time he couldn't describe what he was feeling but told his wife Irene he half expected to see the boogey man in either the bedroom closet or the right front corner of the living room. They painted the interior, and the move into their new home was without incident. As the months passed, Irene decided to replace the kitchen curtains.

Part of the appeal of their new home was the classic 1940s kitchen with lots of chrome on the countertops. While dated, all of the window treatments in their new home were obviously of high quality and quite likely were expensive when purchased. That did not save them from disposal. All were discarded with the exception of the kitchen curtains. Shielded from sunlight, they had held their color remarkably well and their ornate embroidery complimented the room. After a few washings, however, they regrettably began to show their age, and Irene replaced them.

Irene had noticed some difficult to explain events and uncomfortable feelings at various times throughout their home. Money in the form of old coins would appear on windowsills, furniture and counter tops. On occasion an unknown perfume would permeate the kitchen, and the family cat at times jumped to avoid a wreath that literally flew off the wall toward the hapless feline. The day that Irene removed the kitchen curtains and replaced them seemed to be like any other until Irene placed the old curtains in the trash.

The curtains framed the window above the sink and a matching set were on the kitchen door that led to the backyard. Irene, home alone that day from her job, replaced all with newly purchased curtains. She then proceeded out the kitchen door, placed the old curtains into a garbage can, and gathered some herbs from her garden to use later that day. When she attempted to enter the kitchen from outside she discovered the kitchen door would not open more than a few inches. She walked around to the front porch and entered through the front entrance, which was not locked. When she reached the kitchen, she was shocked to discover that the kitchen door had been locked from the inside! No one else was home that day but something had locked the door using the chain door lock but leaving the deadbolt lock undisturbed.

Out of frustration Irene spoke to the departed Mrs. Preston and informed her that her time had passed and it was now their (the Linells') house and kitchen. That afternoon Irene informed her husband that as incredible as it may seem, she believed that Mrs. Preston had locked the door in retaliation for the demise of her once-expensive kitchen curtains.

A short time later, Irene was returning home following an afternoon shift at her job. It was in mid-year, one of those very hot and humid Greene County evenings in late June. Irene had forgotten her house keys that day. Since it was a Saturday, she believed that her husband might still be awake. She was dismayed to discover that Albert, along with their dog, had retired early that night to the comfort of the master bedroom which featured a window air conditioner. The window unit was loud enough that it drowned out the sound of Irene knocking on the door and ringing the doorbell. She tried to contact him by cellphone but Albert was so soundly asleep he could not hear the telephone ring overtop of the air conditioner. Irene had to resort to breaking into her own home by squeezing through an open window on the front porch.

The next day she detailed her previous night's adventure to Albert and they both were amused by the fact that neither he nor the dog heard her beating on the front door in an attempt to wake him. A few days later a brass key appeared on a plant stand situated on an enclosed porch just off the kitchen, right beside the door recently locked from the inside. Albert had not changed the lock when they moved in, and since it fit the lock on the kitchen door each thought the other had found the key and placed it on the plant stand.

Several days passed before Albert asked Irene where she had found the key for the door. Only then did Irene tell him that she had not placed the key where it could be found but she had assumed he had. Dumbfounded, they both quickly thanked Mrs. Preston for leaving the key and accepted it as a peace offering and an acknowledgement that the house was now their property.

Albert Linell had his share of more odd experiences as well. He never entirely put to rest the feeling that there was something unusual about the right front corner of their living room. At first it was nothing other than a feeling, but then Albert began catching a fleeting glimpse of a dark shadow along the wall. It became a regular feature. Although appearances were intermittent, they occurred over such a long period of time he was able to make out the shadowy silhouette: it was a large spectral dog.

The dog came and went as it pleased and periodically stood across the street next to their neighbor's car. At other times it roamed up and down the sidewalk, manifesting at one end of the street and usually moving in a northern direction. Albert found the sightings to be very disturbing but not frightening and eventually he was able to see the specter coming and going from the front corner of their house directly into the living room wall. Irene eventually began to see the black canine as well and agreed that she spotted it entering and leaving the house through the wall.

During this time Irene frequently babysat one of their grandchildren, a bright lad of three years of age. One day the child was in the living room watching television while seated in a large chair. Irene was washing breakfast dishes and noticed the boy was being very quiet. She went to the living room to check on him. What she saw was alarming: the living room couch and chair had been rearranged. The furniture was well made and heavy and would have been nearly impossible for the boy to have moved.

Summoning her sternest grandmotherly tone, she asked the boy if he had rearranged the room. He assured her that he had not, so she asked again. He repeated that he had not moved the furniture. A third inquiry solicited the same response, so Irene demanded to know if he hadn't moved the furniture then who had? His reply: "The black thing that lives in the wall."

A few weeks passed without incident and the boy continued to visit his grandparents frequently. He usually liked to help his grandmother with day-to-day tasks around the house, including the laundry. Eventually he began to refuse to go all the way to the bottom of the basement steps, saying that there was a monster behind the furnace and he didn't like it.

Knowing that children at times can become fearful of corners, closets, crawlspaces and even the space behind furnaces, Irene was not overly concerned. Thinking that he would eventually overcome his fear of the monster behind the furnace, Irene decided to just let things run their course and surely the boy eventually would overcome his fear. He did not; and he began to refer to the monster as a man.

In an attempt to help the boy overcome his anxiety, Irene asked him to describe the man. Her grandson then referred to the man as "Mr. Paintbrush," who was an unhappy and crabby older man. Mr. Paintbrush seemed to be unhappy all the time and was especially unhappy about some damage that had been done to the house. Part of the damage included the never-repaired basement door. The incident that led to the still existing hole in the door was described in great detail by the three-year-old. It seemed that Mr. Paintbrush was moving furniture in the basement with another, younger man (whom the boy also described in detail) when the door was accidentally damaged. This infuriated Mr. Paintbrush, and he continued to remain angry.

The child told the story in such detail that Irene became alarmed and called Albert at work. She asked him what he thought they should do. They both realized that there had been an actual Mr. Paintbrush: John Preston, the previous owner of their home, now deceased. He was well known for his trade as reflected by the nickname their grandson gave him.

65

At the time a local newspaper, now defunct, had published a historical photograph of three men from Waynesburg who hosted a well-attended public event. One of them was the previous owner of the Linells' house, John Preston. Albert suggested that Irene show the boy the newspaper picture. Upon seeing it, he pointed at the man and identified him as Mr. Paintbrush. The Linells had no photographs of John Preston and were not acquainted with him other than they had purchased his house. Other than the day they met with John Preston at their attorney's office to finalize the purchase of their new home, they had no dealings with him.

Their grandson had been born after Preston's death. There is no explanation of how the boy knew the story of how the door was damaged, nor could anyone explain how he identified a deceased man from a newspaper photograph. Unless, of course, Mr. Paintbrush really was behind the furnace.

The Waynesburg haunted apartments

Numerous reports have been made by tenants of a well-known apartment complex that the building is haunted. One resident identified only as "Scared" has had at least one encounter with a ghostly man named Andrew, who sometimes appears and other times is only heard saying, "My name is Andrew and I will not hurt you."

Other tenants and visitors have had frightful experiences such as hearing screams, being pulled out of bed, seeing entities walking around, witnessing floating objects and hearing voices in the stairways. These stories piqued my interest, and I was able to interview two people, current residents, who were willing to share their experiences.

Carmen (not her real name) has been a tenant for more than several years. In December of 2012, shortly after moving in, she noticed an intermittent cold feeling while in her apartment. Often this feeling was accompanied by a sensation of a cold breeze as if someone were very close and walking past.

After these experiences, Carmen often would have difficulty sleeping, and would spend the night on her couch. From this vantage point on several occasions she watched blue and green haze form on the ceiling. The haze shimmered and shifted similar to the Northern Lights, but never dropped toward the floor.

Later Carmen also experienced an unseen hand lifting her covers and exposing her feet and legs. All phenomena seemed to be active most often between midnight and 3 AM.

The following June she decided to try and put a stop to the mysterious events. She initiated a "cast out prayer," in which she asked whatever was visiting her home to stop bothering her. She spoke to them as if they were people present in the room, and she promised to peacefully co-exist if they would simply stop making their presence known to her. She also prayed for protection.

The prayer worked, for the interaction with her ceased.

Carmen also suspected her son may have seen something as well. A toddler when they moved in, he began playing with an unseen friend and holding conversations with the invisible person. If Carmen asked whom he was talking to, the boy would point in the direction he was talking and laugh. The interactions with the invisible friend began soon after he was old enough to sit up on his own and continued until he was three years of age.

During this time Carmen also heard music, although it was difficult to determine its origin. It sounded like drumming, especially the rhythmic patterns that resembled Native American drumming. When she was in the apartment the drumming sounded like it was in the hallway, but upon opening the door it seemed to come from the stairway. No one was ever in the hallway or on the stairs. She mentioned it to one of her neighbors who had lived there for several years and was told that other residents had similar experiences to hers and had heard the drumming as well. It was his opinion, as well as that of other residents, that the complex had been built very near the site of an old Native American village. To this day Carmen still experiences the unexplained cold breezes but now they no longer usher in a feeling of uneasiness.

Another resident, Valerie (not her real name) resides in an apartment that at one time had been occupied by her mother. Valerie's mother told her that some kind of entity frequented her home and seemed to enjoy slapping her on the back of the head.

As her mother was moving out and Valerie was moving in, a friend of the family who knew nothing of the head slapping spirit stopped by to say hello. As they chatted, their friend suddenly jumped and when asked what was wrong stated she thought something had slapped her on the back of the head.

About a week later Valerie's son stopped by to use her computer, and after a short time called to his mother. When she got up to check on him he was outside the room because he too had been slapped on the back of the head by an unseen hand. From that point onward when her son spent the night he did not sleep in the bedroom because he believed there was "something wrong with the room."

Since then, Valerie's grandchildren have also refused to go into the room alone.

Another friend reported seeing the apparition of a man standing in the kitchen dressed in what looked like clothing from the early 1800s.

On other occasions Valerie's window blinds will close themselves, someone invisible will sit behind her on the bed, a doll that has to be squeezed tightly to talk will do so inside the closet despite being packed away in a box in the middle of the night, unintelligible whispering voices are heard, shadows are seen lurking in the apartment, and once a smoky vapor came from beneath the furnace and went out through the wall below the window.

Shadow people are dark human-like figures often wearing coats and hats. They haunt buildings, homes and land. Credit: John Weaver.

There are reports that some rooms in the complex are difficult to keep occupied because tenants refuse to remain in them due to hauntings. Some speculate the land on which the apartments were constructed was once some type of burial ground, but I could not find conclusive proof of those claims.

However, it is an area of documented Native American activity, and it is possible that a burial ground and/or village site was destroyed during construction.

69

CHAPTER 8

THE GHOST OF FRANK BRYAN

Prior to the completion of I-79 in 1975, Waynesburg had many of the familiar components that make up the business districts of many small towns across rural America. There was a Coca-Cola bottling plant, several mom and pop corner grocery stores, two bakeries, two creameries, three hardware stores, a furrier, several farm-related enterprises and other long established, successful businesses. One such business was the Waynesburg Sanitary Dairy Company, also known as Bryan's Dairy after the family that founded the business.

Located on East High Street in Waynesburg, Bryan's Dairy was renowned for its ice cream and cottage cheese, both produced on site. To say their ice cream was premium would be an understatement: it was high in fat and flavor. The same could be said of their cottage cheese, and Bryan's chocolate milk was rich and thick enough to be compared to melted ice cream. Untold numbers of Greene County students had

Bryan's milk with their brown bag and/or school lunches, drinking from distinctive square paper cartons with flat tops.

Bryan's Dairy was not only known for its products, but also for its ability to cause traffic problems as well. When traveling up High Street on delivery day, it was not uncommon to see trucks backed into their loading dock which faced the street. At times tankers would nearly obstruct the entire street, allowing traffic to pass in single file only in space normally used for parking. Later in the day, or especially on weekends in warm weather people literally would come by the carload from miles around for ice cream cones. Parking would be at a premium on both sides of the street, and the large numbers of pedestrians would force passers-by to slow down.

Their reputation for quality products and demand for hand-dipped ice cream resulted in many jobs for local youth. Known as dairy boys/girls, many an arm was pressed into service at Bryan's. Their retail space featured a large hand-dipping cabinet, a dipping well where the scoops resided and were kept clean until their next use, a large shelf that provided storage for paper containers of various sizes for milkshakes, hand-dipped pints and quarts, and for a time a large root beer barrel. The walls were block, smooth and finished with a baked glaze that allowed for cleaning. Also present were milkshake mixers, the flavor board, and cones ready to be filled. At times it would be so busy that three or more employees would have a difficult time keeping up with demand. At other times, nearing closing time, it would be eerily quiet with no customers in sight for a considerable length of time. It was into those quiet evenings that the ghost of Frank Bryan appeared.

There were two dairy boys named Tom and Jerry (not their real names) who not only went to high school together but also frequently closed the store together. They were friends of mine, and often on Friday or Saturday nights I would stop in before they closed to see which of the local watering holes either of them might be visiting on their way home from work. Both young men were well known and popular with their classmates. Both were very intelligent, but Tom was more outgoing than Jerry. Tom, in fact, could be a bit of a prankster at times... nothing hurtful or dangerous, just good fun.

One evening I stopped by at dusk when Jerry was about to go from the store into the milk plant in order to restock the coolers and shelves for the next day's business. He seemed reluctant to go, so much so that I inquired as to what was wrong. All I could get out of Jerry was that he didn't like going into the milk plant alone because it was "creepy," and out the door he went. Tom immediately burst into laughter and informed me that for the past few nights when they had worked together he had been telling Jerry the milk plant was haunted by Frank Bryan. Tom then asked me if I would help him weave the tale of the ghost of Frank Bryan and its alleged prowling throughout the building. I agreed to join the fun and help Tom with his ghost story.

I worked at a neighboring business and could clearly see Bryan's Dairy through the windows where I worked or from where I frequently parked. Tom would tell Jerry about shadows he had seen in the milk plant, or strange sounds and footsteps he had heard. I would say I had seen someone looking out the window or standing on the loading dock when no one was in the building or when the store was closed. We laid it on as we went; any ghost-like thing we could think of was told to Jerry. The recurring theme was that Frank Bryan was angry and wanted us – and him – out of the building.

This went on for a short amount of time until one Friday evening after I stopped by. After my arrival Tom sent Jerry into the milk plant, as was customary, for Tom had seniority. Jerry returned with the needed inventory and said something along the lines that the milk plant was haunted, and he was afraid of the ghost of Frank Bryan. Tom and I immediately burst into laughter, and breathlessly let Jerry in on the prank: we made it all up, there was no ghost, and Frank Bryan wasn't angry with anyone.

At that very moment paper cups and ice cream containers flew off the shelf behind the counter as if tossed by an unseen hand. None of us were near the shelf, nobody touched it, nor was there any explanation of how and why the paper products flew off the shelf. The doors were closed, and there was no wind. The shelf was level. There were no proverbial strings attached to the cups and containers.

While I never learned for certain exactly what was the cause, that was the last time I participated in a paranormal practical joke.

CHAPTER 9

MYSTERY PEOPLE AND BLACK-EYED PEOPLE

Our walk through this life, for those who take time to observe it, is filled with wonders that sometimes defy our ability to describe them. The serene beauty of trees, the bright colors of fall, the undying admiration and loyalty of the family dog, the air of privacy surrounding the aloof house cat. There are birds singing and darting about, wildlife of every shape, size and description imaginable, and insects that emerge from the ground once every 17 years to sing, mate and die. Science can tell you the genus and species of the lightning bug but can't tell you what makes it blink on warm summer evenings.

We blunder about amidst all the grandeur that is nature, many times caught up in matters that seem important at the moment. As we focus upon work, sports, clothing, celebrities or the politically correct cause du jour, we get out of the habit of simply observing our surroundings. Since seeing is believing, for many there is much about this existence that is missed simply because those who could be witnessing it are not paying attention.

Others are more observant, or perhaps are tuned to a different wavelength. That is not to say one is more correct than the other, but rather some are more aware of their environment and less easily distracted than others. A case in point is Marco (not his real name) who, upon hearing that I was doing research for this book, was eager to assist with finding individuals who had had paranormal experiences and were willing to share them. As work progressed, Marco told me of an odd experience with a "mystery person" that he had in Franklin Township just outside Waynesburg.

The weird woman

Marco stopped early one morning at a local pharmacy to pick up some items he needed for later that day. It was just after 9 AM, and the pharmacy had just opened. He purchased the items he needed, climbed into his vehicle to leave and began to back out of his parking spot. He noticed an individual standing in the drive-thru lane facing his direction. It was a woman of average height, dressed in conservative business attire and holding a dark leather briefcase. It struck him as a little odd that an individual would be standing and blocking access to the pharmacy's drive-thru pick-up lane, so he lowered his passenger side window to ask if she needed assistance. She replied that she did not and was waiting for her ride. Her demeanor was unusual: emotionless, almost stoic. Her blonde hair, poker straight and neat, framed a pair of bright, piercing blue eyes which peered unblinkingly at Marco. Her clothing, like her hair, was picture perfect and unrumpled; her shoes shiny and clean.

Since the woman seemed to be aware of her surroundings and had stated she was waiting for her ride, Marco assumed all was well and proceeded east out of town. He had traveled perhaps three-quarters of a mile and was passing the community aquatic park and swimming pool when he noticed a pedestrian walking westward along the very same route. As he got a better look at the pedestrian he was stunned to see it was the woman he had just seen at the pharmacy drive-thru. Unbelieving, he slowed to get a better look. It was indeed the same person: Marco recognized the clothes, briefcase and straight blonde hair.

Given that the fastest recorded speed for a human being on foot is 27.44 miles per hour, it simply was not possible for the blonde to have traveled three quarters of a mile on foot in the three minutes it took Marco to pass her heading east.

Muttering to himself in disbelief, he continued on his way to run some errands. He returned to Waynesburg later that morning, still questioning what he had seen. As he traveled toward the center of town he passed a used car lot and noticed someone standing between two shiny cars facing the street as if watching traffic. Marco looked over and was shocked to see the same woman. This time she was looking directly at him with her incredibly blue eyes and face that showed no emotion.

Marco found the experience that day to be quite unnerving. He was not fearful of the person he saw, but more of what she may have been. Was it a case of identical twins unknown to him who were playing an elaborate prank? Perhaps she was a female version of the famous Men In Black (MIB), who are said to harass and intimidate those who have seen unidentified flying objects or reported cryptids such as Bigfoot or the famous Mothman of Point Pleasant, West Virginia.

Had he encountered what some have called an Aryan or Nordic alien? In ufology Nordic aliens are humanoid extraterrestrials purported to come from the Pleiades and resemble Nordic-Scandinavian humans. If so, what was her interest in pharmacies, used cars, or especially *him*? Since he had not seen anything like her before, nor has he since, Marco claims that in his opinion the encounter was strictly due to the fact that he assisted with the research for this book.

As far-fetched as that might sound, it's quite a plausible explanation. Many researchers find that as soon as they start inquiring into the peculiarities of the paranormal, something odd happens to them, as though to send the message that yes, a strange world exists alongside ours.

The woman did not have the usual characteristics of a Woman in Black. These human-like figures are dressed in black, have black hair and dark eyes. Something is out of kilter with them, as though someone in a laboratory made a faulty imitation of a human being.

Angels have bright blue eyes, but she did not fit the characteristics of angels, either. Angels usually show up in response to a need, such as a problem or crisis that needs solving.

She was and is, a mystery figure.

The Black-Eyed People

Enter Justin (not his real name), who also was a great help to me in my research. Justin is fairly well known in some circles, and lives a comfortable, routine and some would say "normal" life. Justin has worked in sales for years, and some say he has an eye for facial details and body language that most salespeople gain over the years to help them "read" clients and make sales.

After he started assisting me, Justin had two encounters with Black-Eyed People.

Black-Eyed People are one of the newest entities on the paranormal block – at least in times of reporting – but their roots are centuries old. The current phenomenon dates to the 1990s, and is credited to a man named Brian Bethel, who posted an account of his experience on the internet more than a year after it happened.

Bethel said he left his home in Abilene, Texas at about 9:30 PM one night to run an errand at the downtown shopping center. He parked his car and, while the engine was still running, he was suddenly approached by two boys who seemed quite odd. He gauged them to be between 10 and 14 years of age. The taller of the two wore a pullover hooded shirt with a gray checkered pattern; he had olive-colored skin and curly,

Black-Eyed Kids. Credit: Laume Conroy.

medium-length brown hair. The second boy had pale skin "with a trace of freckles," and pale orange hair; he was wearing a hooded shirt that was light green in color. He looked quite nervous. Bethel assumed they were going to hit him up for money. He rolled his window down a crack.

The taller boy said they wanted to see the movie *Mortal Kombat* that was playing at the shopping center theater, but they had forgotten their money. They did not want any from him, however – they wanted him to give them a ride to their home to collect money and come back.

Something about the kids literally chilled Bethel's blood. Glancing at the theater marquee, he saw that the last showing of *Mortal Kombat* had started one hour earlier, and there was no way the boys could catch the rest of the film.

As he hesitated, the taller boy grew more insistent and demanded that Bethel let them into the car. It was then that Bethel noticed that the youth had solid black eyes. He floored the gas pedal and sped off.

After that, Black-Eyed Kids stories started popping up everywhere. There were patterns to the encounters. People were often approached by one or more BEKs in parking lots, demanding to get inside and be taken somewhere. BEKs also came to people's doors late at night, asking to be let in. Sometimes they had bizarre requests. One young BEK knocked on a door and asked the residents for ketchup for his apple.

BEKs then mutated into adults, and both children and adults made aggressive approaches to people. More than anything, they seemed to want contact – any kind of contact, eye or physical. People who had encounters with Black-Eyed People reported ill effects afterwards: sudden onsets of illness, runs of bad luck. It was as though they were some sort of Grim Reaper sowing misfortune.

Skeptics were quick to jump in and dismiss the entire phenomenon, pointing out that no one had heard of Black-Eyed Kids (or adults) prior to Bethel's story. Bethel said he waited about a year to post it, out of uncertainty over its reception. As experiencers are quick to learn, ridicule runs high.

As we mentioned in the introduction, mysterious phenomena remain consistent through the ages, but adapt to changes in society and technology, and acquire new names. The Black-Eyed People have a great deal in common with Men In Black, who harass mostly UFO researchers and witnesses. They, too, exhibit bizarre behavior and leave behind them a toxic trail of mishaps and illness. MIBs came along with the modern UFO era post-World War II – but their roots also go much deeper.

Looking into history, we find many accounts of "dark ghosts" or "dark mystery people" who have the same quirky behavior – appropriate for the times – and ill effects. A century or more ago, people did not call these things "Black-Eyed People," but a rose is a rose is a rose. Going back even further, we can trace similarities to the black monks, phantom monks and phantom nuns: sinister cowled or hooded figures. Even stories of the "man in black" said to be the Devil fit the mold. The bottom line: they are dark figures with dark or black eyes who are up to no good. Yesterday's hooded black monk is today's hooded kid or adult.

Justin's run-ins with Black-Eyed People

Justin's first encounter occurred while he was sitting in traffic in a construction zone near the town of Carmichaels in eastern Greene County. Two younger adults, a man and a woman, were in a car behind him. The driver had been tailgating Justin until they were stopped. What really caught Justin's eye was the flash of a bright blue light in the passenger side mirror of his truck. Thinking it might be a police car he searched the mirror to determine if there was in fact a police officer approaching with lights and siren.

At that point he noticed the bright blue light again, only to realize it was coming from the dashboard of the car behind him. The man had long hair which obscured his face as he was looking downward, but the woman's hair was parted in the middle and revealed her face. Her countenance, according to Justin, could be described as stern or even angry. Her eyes looked like "two black holes," and she was clutching a device in her right hand and pointing it at his vehicle. It looked rectangular and emitted a series of bright flashes similar to LED lights: red, green, yellow and blue.

Justin was staring into the mirror trying to ascertain what the angry-looking young woman was pointing in his direction and what she might be doing. At that point their eyes met as she saw him staring at her in the truck mirror and she hurriedly hid the blinking device from his sight.

Traffic began to crawl forward, and the long-haired driver of the car began tapping his horn as if to get Justin's attention. Justin signaled a left turn toward Waynesburg while the Black-Eyed Woman and her companion signaled a right turn for Carmichaels. As they crept toward their turning points the driver hung his head out the car window and started shouting "Hey.... hey.... hey.... hey..." as if to get Justin's attention. He ignored them and drove home; he later described the encounter as very disturbing.

Justin's experience has some weird parallels that are hard to explain. On July 20, 2015, two friends of Rosemary's were on their way from Point Pleasant, West Virginia to their home in Beaufort, North Carolina. Joey Madia and his daughter, Jolie, had met up with some other paranormal investigators in Point Pleasant. Joey and his wife, Tonya, a sensitive, are veteran investigators, and Jolie is a sensitive as well.

They had an encounter on the road with a Man In Black driving an old black car. He was holding a strange-looking, brick-sized black box in one hand. He was pressing it against his face like a man would an electric razor – although it clearly was no razor. As they approached a tunnel, the MIB shot forward at high speed and disappeared.

Joey commented that the box reminded him of "phreaking phone boxes," which were popular in the 1960s, especially among young people. The boxes would fool the telephone company about long distance calls, so that they could be made free.

In both cases, it seems some sort of electronic manipulation might have been going on.

Justin's Black-Eyed Kid encounter

Later a BEK (Black-Eyed Kid) came to the door of the Waynesburg store where Justin was employed at the time, allegedly looking for a restroom. Justin was the only one present. Since business was slow that day, he was watching the proverbial world go by on High Street. He noticed two youths, a boy and a girl, walking up the opposite side of the street. As they passed businesses the boy would open doors but not go through them while the girl stood by or sometimes sat on the curb.

Justin had the impression the young man was opening doors and asking a question of those occupying the buildings. The two soon approached Justin's door, and following the same pattern the young man opened it. Justin described him as medium in height and about

Cover of David Weatherly's authoritative work on Black-Eyed Children and Kids.
Credit: Sam Shearon.

13 or 14 years old. He was not tan as if he had been outside much, but rather his skin was a pale, sort of ashen gray/tan. His hair was curly, and his clothes were nothing extraordinary. His eyes, however, were "black as coal" with no visible whites or pupils. Looking in his eyes, Justin said, was like "staring into a black abyss where the pupils should have been."

"Do you have a restroom?" the young man asked. "Do you have a restroom? May I come in? Do you have a restroom? May I use your rest room?"

Justin was fearful of the young man with the coal-black eyes. He was momentarily unable to respond, perhaps to the shock of once again seeing a Black-Eyed Person. Quickly recovering, Justin suspected what the young man really wanted was access to the building. His request to use the restroom was denied. Justin suggested he use one of the public restrooms he had already passed, which seemed to anger the young Black-Eyed Kid, but he and his female companion went on their way.

Justin had never been a believer in the stories of BEKs but now wondered if they might be true. In keeping with many tales of BEK encounters, Justin had some misfortune after his encounters. After the traffic encounter, he suddenly became quite ill, requiring extensive and expensive medical tests to determine the cause.

When he returned home after work and told a family member about his BEK visitor seeking a restroom, one member became violently ill within four hours and was quite sick for the next 48 hours. While it very well could have been caused by a virus or perhaps food poisoning, no one else in the family became sick at that time.

High strangeness

I have had my own odd experiences while assisting Rosemary with her work and research in Greene County. They include the following:

Within days of Justin relating his story about the Black-Eyed People behind him in traffic, I was traveling on Route 119 in Fayette

County. One end of the lower radiator hose on my truck somehow managed to detach itself from the radiator. The clamp was as tight as it was on the day it was installed; in fact, I had to loosen it considerably to reconnect it to the radiator. There was absolutely nothing else wrong with the vehicle, but the hose, complete with tight hose clamp, managed to detach itself and cause a complete and sudden loss of coolant. Luckily, I was able to park at a nearby Kmart, purchase anti-freeze, reinstall the hose and continue on my way.

On another occasion, I found dead birds placed on my windshield wipers on cold, dry, frostless nights. The birds were either freshly killed and were stuck to my windshield by their own frozen blood, or had water poured over them, freezing them in place.

I once found a new, unopened package of automotive brake hardware in the bed of my truck. Shortly thereafter, oddly enough, I had brake problems and had to have the vehicle repaired.

The fuse box cover of my truck disappeared. It was found in a box – in Connecticut, hundreds of miles away, at the residence of, you guessed it, Rosemary Ellen Guiley. I have never been to Rosemary's home and cannot explain how it got there. She found it when she was moving boxes around in her basement. Hearing an unusual rattle in one, she looked inside and found the fuse box cover.

I attempted to email a rather unusual picture taken at night to a family member living out of state. What I emailed was a color photograph of a building. What he received was a children's crayon drawing of a bald eagle.

When investigating stories we had heard about haunted Rices Landing, which we explore in the later in this book, I visited the Greene River Trail at the landing on one cool Saturday afternoon in November. There was no one about, but I did encounter one elderly gentleman dressed in black. No one knew I was on the trail other than my wife and youngest daughter.

As I passed the old man I said hello, to which he replied, "People that come down here and poke around often get hurt. If I were you I would be careful." As he shuffled off, I attempted many times to get his picture with my digital camera, but the device simply refused to focus. I did get one picture when the man was several hundred feet away from me that shows no details of his appearance.

Was he a mystery figure warning me off my research? Similar things have happened to other investigators of the paranormal, UFOs and mysterious phenomena.

On more occasions than I can recall when trying to communicate with Rosemary, there was a complete and total technology failure. Emails were never received, computers locked up or crashed, texts vanished into Never Never Land – just the ones I was sending to Rosemary. Otherwise, my computer functioned normally.

Phone messages are received that are nothing more than unusual sounds. It has become a rule of thumb in our household that when communicating with Rosemary one must expect electrical problems, phone malfunctions, car problems, and other annoying activity. While many of these events could very well have easy explanations, there is no denying the fact that they occur in clusters either when Rosemary is coming to Greene County to research or we have been discussing the book. In our home we call this the Guiley Effect.

And stay away from that Guiley woman!

When we decided to write this book, initially I discussed it with no one other than my wife and youngest daughter. We had barely started when one evening I was walking toward home and was approached by a man who told me in no uncertain terms that whatever I discovered in my research, I was not to "give it to that woman," but instead I was to turn it over to him. I ignored his suggestion.

On a more humorous note, by far one of my favorite unusual occurrences involves another family member. This person once delivered a scathing commentary on people who research the paranormal in general, and Rosemary Ellen Guiley in particular. According to this person I had become a victim of mind control exercised by Rosemary, who for reasons unknown simply decided to travel hundreds of miles to Greene County and place ideas, events and stories of the paranormal into people's heads, including mine. This paranormal research was all a load of hooey and should be ignored! These things simply do not happen, period, paragraph, exclamation point.

Within days I received a telephone call from this very same person asking me to walk through a house he was thinking of buying because he had encountered something in the basement that defied explanation, and he was afraid the house was haunted. I suggested he purchase the house and live there because, after all, these things simply do not happen, period, paragraph, exclamation point.

Chapter 10

Rices Landing: A Paranormal Hotspot

Rices Landing is a small borough that hugs a western bank curve on the mighty Monongahela River, about 17 miles east of Waynesburg and 50 miles south of Pittsburgh. There are fewer than 500 people living in its 583 acres, which include Pumpkin Run Park and the Greene River Trail.

Many people find Rices Landing a spooky place, and for good reason – the area boasts a wide variety of paranormal phenomena, is related to a tragic murder and is the site of one of Greene County's most famous legendary hauntings.

Historical background

In the 19th century, Rices Landing was an important river port and coal mining center. Huge paddlewheel steamboats docked there, and coal boats ferried their loads up and down the river. In the early 20th century, coal magnate H.C. Frick of Pittsburgh acquired one of the deep shaft mines, the Dilworth Mine, and many of the lots in Rices Landing, including two blocks between Second Street and the ferry landing. Most of the coal mines are shut down today. The huge industrial riverboats no longer ply the waters. The area is full of coal spoil, the waste rocks that accumulate from the mining process.

The borough still has much of its original Victorian and turn-of-the-20th-century architecture, comprising a historic district that is now on the National Register of Historic Places.

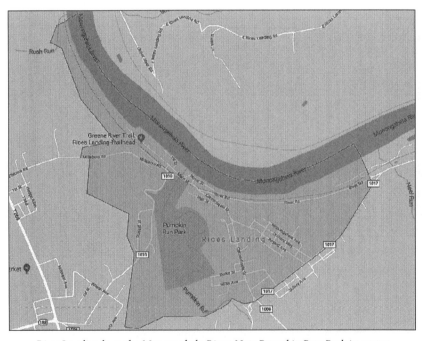

Rices Landing hugs the Monongahela River. Note Pumpkin Run Park in center.

A tragic murder

On October 5, 1973, eight-year-old Debra Lynne Makel, a bright and accomplished student, got off her school bus and began the walk up the long drive to her family's home off Ferncliff Road near Rices Landing. She did this every weekday, and no one ever worried that anything bad would happen to her. She wore a pretty green dress and carried a cute little pink purse.

Debbie was spotted walking that afternoon by several persons: her two brothers, ages 11 and 12, who were out in the neighborhood selling magazine subscriptions; a neighbor; and a jogger. But she never made it to her family home, vanishing somewhere along the driveway. By evening, her now alarmed family called the police and began searching for her. Clearly, she was not out playing. About 180 people joined the search, combing through the woods.

Two days later, on October 7, two of Debbie's cousins were searching through Pumpkin Run Park near the family home and spotted something green poking through the forest debris on the ground. There, buried in a shallow grave, was little Debbie's body. She had been raped and strangled with a piece of twine. The brutal murder of this sweet little girl shocked the county.

Despite the collection of DNA samples and thousands of leads, Debbie's murder remains unsolved, more than 40 years later. The DNA samples were never matched to any in databases.

An unsolved murder evokes a heavy sadness. There is never closure for the family or the community. No one is ever brought to justice. No one ever learns how the crime was committed, or why. It hangs in limbo.

Today, curiosity seekers still poke through the tangled underbrush at the approximate spot where Debbie's body was found and wonder if her spirit remains on the land.

The haunting of Stovepipe

Smack in the middle of Rices Landing is Pumpkin Run Park, famous for a haunting legend of a headless ghost named Stovepipe who comes when you call his name – or so the story goes.

There are several versions of the legend, which dates to the early 1800s when violence was breaking out over attempts to unionize coal workers.

According to one version, a union activist was named Stovepipe Kelly because he always wore a stovepipe hat. One night he was chased by coal mine owners into the hilly area now known as Pumpkin Run Park. Kelly raced along the winding road in his buggy. When he hit a sharp curve aptly called Horseshoe Bend, he was thrown from the buggy, which ran over him and decapitated him. He was found the next morning with his neck stretched out and his head missing. It was never recovered.

In another version of the legend, Kelly was having an affair with the wife of one of the owners of the coal mines. One rainy night he was sneaking home and took the road down the hillside as a short cut. At the bottom of the hill, he was surprised by the angry husband, who hit the buggy and threw Kelly off. He was run over and decapitated. When his body was found, the head was missing.

In yet another version, a young man – not Stovepipe Kelly – was driving his buggy on a rainy night in the early 1800s and took a short cut down the hill. When he reached the railroad tracks at Pumpkin Run and started across the tracks, a speeding train came along and struck the buggy, overturning it. The young man catapulted out and was run over by the train and decapitated. The ghost placed a piece of stovepipe where his head had been.

Over the years, more modern versions of the Stovepipe Kelly story developed. According to one, the decapitated victim was a young boy who was hit by a train while playing on the tracks. According to another, the victim was a teenager who drove down the hill one night

Horseshoe Bend where the legendary Stovepipe Kelly lost his head. Credit: R.E. Guiley.

after leaving a party. He failed to negotiate the curve at Horseshoe Bend and his car veered off into rocks. He was thrown out and landed in a stovepipe chimney. This version was later given some credence because of a rusted, wrecked car in the woods nearby.

According to legend, the ghost of Stovepipe can be summoned at night, especially rainy nights, and at Halloween. Drive down the winding road of the park and at Horseshoe Bend shout, "Stovepipe, Stovepipe, Stovepipe!" If Stovepipe shows up, he will be looking for his missing head – and might take the one of the person who is calling him.

One local young man told us he and his friends – about six in number – once liked to go to Pumpkin Run Park to see if they could scare up ole Stovepipe. One year, after calling Stovepipe's name, they observed a peculiar orange light in the distance. At first, they thought it might be a light on a house or building that had just come on – but the light started to sway back and forth and grow bigger and brighter, as though it were approaching them. The motion looked like a lantern held by someone who was walking.

After watching the light for several minutes, the youths suddenly panicked and decided not to stick around to see what might happen. They jumped in their cars and sped away.

The Greene River Trail

Running alongside the Monongahela River through Rices Landing and beyond is the Greene River Trail for walking and biking. It is 5.2 miles long, and ends in Crucible, a nearby town with another tragedy that we shall soon relate.

On the surface the trail looks peaceful, but many hikers soon have odd experiences as they go along. One is a powerful, even

The Greene River Trail boasts plenty of paranormal activity. Credit: R.E. Guiley.

overwhelming, urge to jump off the bank on the side of the trail into the river. One man told us he suddenly heard "a thousand whispering voices" urging him to jump. The voices rushed past him and seemed to go into the river themselves.

Shadow figures are also seen along the trail. Tall, skinny and solid black, they lurk on both sides of the trail, suddenly popping into view as a person passes them. If you turn around to look back, they are not visible. They seem to be watching people – and they want others to know it.

One of the features of the trail is a welded steel sculpture of a hiker. According to eyewitnesses, the sculpture seems to have gained the attention of things unknown. At various times chanting can be heard near it, but never quite plainly enough for the listener to understand what is being said.

Chanting sounds emanate from steel hiker sculpture. Credit: R.E. Guiley.

On one occasion a cyclist on the trail encountered what looked like a patch of fog several feet off the ground but against the trunk of a tree. As the witness watched, the fog began to slide down the tree toward the ground. It was approximately two feet square, and once it came into contact with the ground it slid across the trail and vanished.

The haunting of public buildings

Locals have also reported that at least three borough buildings are haunted, so much so that from time to time regional paranormal investigators have set up shop in an attempt to ascertain what continues to creep about, stalking the living and making its presence known.

Central to much of the activity is the W. A. Young and Sons Machine Shop, a virtual time capsule of the steam riverboat era. The shop and its foundry existed to provide much needed service and repair to the boats plying the Monongahela. For decades it sat idle; the building and its contents now serve as a snapshot of a long-gone period of local industrialization. Managed by the Greene County Historical Society, its volunteers host visitors and various groups throughout the year.

One volunteer firmly believes the shop is still visited by a now deceased friend who spent literally hundreds of hours there working to preserve the facility. Paranormal investigators are on record saying there may be several spirits frequenting the building, ranging from children to adult men. Recordings have been made that feature a young child's voice saying, "Let me go," as well as the sound of someone whistling. Objects fall for no apparent reason, and investigators caught on video at least one item – a flashlight – rolling off a table by itself.

Another hot spot is the old Rices Landing jail. Last used in the 1940s, at least one unintentional death occurred there when a prisoner succumbed to carbon monoxide produced by a malfunctioning natural gas heater. Investigators called to examine the machine shop also state they detected activity in the jail as well. They are on record as claiming to have communicated with the ghost of a 10-year-old girl who said she liked apple pie.

The fire hall is haunted as well. Firefighters have reported hearing footsteps. Lights turned off are found to be turned on again. Tables and chairs rearrange themselves, and a second-floor curtain is pulled back when no one is present. Ghostly figures have been reported in the building and have been seen by witnesses. At least some of the activity is attributed to the accidental death of a fireman in the 1940s, who was pinned between a fire truck and the building wall.

More paranormal activity

Bigfoot sightings have been reported in the area, including large bipedal figures that are accompanied by black dogs. Witnesses describe them as furry, having sloped shoulders, large heads and long arms. Frequently the dogs are described as having red eyes.

Entities called "jawas" also have been seen in the woods. Named after the beings in the *Star Wars* films, they are small, robed and hooded humanoid creatures with no faces and luminous eyes. They have been seen scurrying and darting among the trees.

Numerous shadow cats also have been seen prowling around the buildings. Perhaps they are the ghosts of feral cats as well as pets from bygone days.

Shadow cats seen in Rices Landing. Credit: Melanie Miller.

97

And in the environs

Not far from Rices Landing, near the town of Crucible, another horrific murder took place. On January 19, 1996, Franklin Delano Virgili Jr., 43, and his girlfriend, Joelene Bowers, 20, were sitting on an I-beam spread across an open abandoned mine shaft, drinking beer. Virgili was angry because Bowers had told the mother of his daughter that he and Bowers were having a relationship.

Virgili pushed Bowers down the 300-foot shaft and tossed her purse and coat after her. He then told a friend he had "taken care" of Bowers. He told others she had fallen down the shaft accidentally.

He was arrested two days later and charged with first-degree murder. He pleaded guilty to avoid a death sentence conviction. He was convicted and sentenced to life in prison; as of 2012 he had lost all appeals.

Divers attempted to recover Bowers' body but could find only one of her arms. The remainder of her corpse was likely submerged and tangled in the water and debris that collects in abandoned shafts.

People who visit the area feel a foreboding atmosphere, perhaps a lingering ghostly trace of the tragic death.

CHAPTER 11

CRAZY HAUNTINGS

The Hartley Inn

For generations South Market Street in Carmichaels has played host to the Hartley Inn. In 1847 Noah Minor Hartley purchased the property from the Jeremiah Davidson estate and the Hartley Inn was born. Passing through ownership by several families, the Hartley Inn currently is owned by Karen Romah and her husband, Phillip.

Karen has spent countless hours in the Hartley Inn kitchen, and it was there where she had her first ghost encounter while cooking at the grill. Without warning, someone blew a puff of air on the back of her neck. Whirling around, she discovered she was entirely alone in the kitchen.

On another occasion, she was working with another employee in the kitchen when a man in a gray pullover shirt walked through the room.

He was thin and visible for only a moment. It was a Saturday and Karen thought he might have been the breadman making his weekly delivery.

Another person was working in the kitchen cooking, and the man had walked right past her. Karen asked if she had seen him. She replied that she had not, but that when she opened the restaurant for the day the morning waitress had seen a man in the kitchen who also wore a gray shirt. Once again, with the exception of Karen and her employee there were no other people in the kitchen. The ghost has also appeared wearing a striped green shirt and has been seen by employees working in different parts of the inn.

The shadowy ghost also has an affection for doing impersonations. One evening at closing time, Karen was alone in the restaurant with her daughter. At the time the kitchen doors had distinctively squeaky hinges; everyone had come to recognize the sound of them opening and closing.

The Hartley Inn, Carmichaels. Credit: R.E. Guiley.

Karen's daughter finished up for the evening and said good-bye, her exit punctuated by the telltale squeaky door. A few minutes later Karen heard the door squeak again and her daughter called out to her.

"What?" Karen responded and then waited in vain for her daughter to reply. Karen left the kitchen and checked the remainder of the restaurant only to realize that her daughter was not in the building. This was the first time the ghost mimicked the living, but it was not the last. Repeatedly the ghost has used other people's voices to fool the living and it seems to enjoy calling out to people who are skeptical of its presence when Karen tells of her experiences.

One of the frequent chores is replenishing the ice supply in the restaurant by carrying buckets of ice cubes up from the basement ice machine. On one occasion Karen delegated this task to a newly hired waitress. Down the steps from the kitchen she went with the ice buckets, only to bolt back up to the kitchen, telling her co-workers that she saw someone in the basement. Even though she continued to work at the Hartley Inn, from that point onward she refused to go into the basement.

Eventually the waitress went on to other things. At one point she returned with her own daughter to visit with Karen. When Karen asked if she ever told her daughter of her experiences with the Hartley ghost, the former waitress reached for her cellphone which had a ghost-hunting app. Once activated it showed two ghosts within the building.

The apparition seems prefer to introduce itself to skeptics by either calling to them by name or blowing a puff of air on the back of their neck; for staff it prefers the more direct approach of becoming visible. Patrons and staff alike are divided on proof of the existence of the haunting host. There are the believers, non-believers and those who have experienced an encounter.

A cook told me of an encounter when first hired; she had heard of the entity but had not yet seen it. As she cooked one morning she saw an unfamiliar person move through the kitchen and go around the corner. Looking to see who it was, she saw no one. The moment she convinced herself that it was all in her imagination, objects flew off the opposite wall from where she was working. The specter put in additional appearances after that as if it wanted to be certain she had seen it.

The Greene Academy of Art

The Greene Academy of Art began as an Episcopal church constructed of stone around 1790, with a brick addition added in 1810. The academy ceased operation in 1893, and subsequent building uses included a Grand Army of the Republic post and apartments. In the 1970s a restoration of the building was completed and since that time it has housed the Greene Academy of Arts and functions as a community center hosting public events and providing tours when scheduled in advance.

Some reports indicate that the Academy plays host to unscheduled visitors as well. A small cemetery was established on site during the building's use as a church. Graves were later moved to the nearby Laurel Point Cemetery, and witnesses have reported seeing shadowy figures moving from the Academy in the direction of Laurel Point Cemetery. It is as if the spirits who once rested in the former church cemetery are looking for their bodies' final resting places now a short distance away. Others have heard disembodied voices and footsteps of unseen people. A group of regional investigators visited the site in 2011 and claimed to have captured voices on recordings as well as unusual activity on at least one video.

The Morrisville Mumbler

The owner of an established business in Morrisville who does not wish to be identified has had two visits from a ghostly, stooped over, disheveled figure of an elderly woman who talked loudly in gibberish. The first encounter occurred in early 2010 when the witness saw what he thought was an unkempt elderly woman enter his establishment. He was working and saw the figure in his peripheral vision walking left to right. She stopped under a ceiling light and began speaking unintelligibly.

Thinking perhaps she was ill or confused, he stopped what he was doing and approached her to offer help. She did not acknowledge his presence and stared off into space. When he drew near she simply vanished.

During summer of that same year she returned to the same area of the store while the owner was on a stepladder changing light bulbs. He described her as slightly built, about five feet tall and guessed her weight at no more than 115 pounds. She wore an old print dress and sweater. Her face was very wrinkled with a protruding jaw and a large nose. Her eyes were slits, as if she were squinting, and her hair was pulled back in a tight bun. She began to speak again in gibberish. He climbed down the ladder and when his feet touched the floor she disappeared.

The store poltergeist

An employee of a neighboring Morrisville business, a variety-type store now closed, described unusual activity during her employment there. Late in the day when customers were absent, merchandise would fly off the shelves on its own. There were also repeated incidents of the doors of the restroom stalls locking themselves, and lights that turned off and on without explanation.

CHAPTER 12

WEIRD WARRIOR TRAIL

Whiteley Township can lay claim to paranormal hot spots as well. The small village of Kirby along Route 19 south of Waynesburg was once a sleepy, closely knit farm community complete with school, post office, store and church. It is in the shadow of the Warrior Trail, a well-known Native American trail that stretches 67 miles from the Monongahela River to what is now Moundsville, West Virginia.

The Warrior Trail predates the European settlement of Pennsylvania by several millennia. It is believed to have been used for 5,000 years by Native Americans traveling to Flint Ridge in Ohio for trading and conferencing. The route was first studied by professors at Waynesburg College in the 1930s. The Warrior Trail offers a hike of great historical interest and marks the divide between the Whiteley Creek and Dunkard Creek watersheds. It is interesting to note that one may traverse the entire width of Greene County on the Warrior Trail and never ford a stream.

The Kirby area has a long history of the unexplained covering a wide range of phenomena. One of its most famous ghosts is the Woman of Lemley Road, said to be the restless spirit of a woman murdered by her abusive husband. Several generations of witnesses are said to have encountered a wispy woman in white along Lemley Road who has a look of horror on her face. She has attempted to enter vehicles. In the days before cars were common she was said to have looked so frightening that carriage drivers lost control of horses panicked by her appearance.

Prior to the 1970s, Kirby periodically hosted unusual phenomena, including strange and unexplained bright lights capable of illuminating entire hillsides; curious small-dog-sized black shadows that scurried in and out of houses and doorways; and a particularly frightening blue devil that leaped about in a barn much to the consternation of kids attempting to complete their farm chores. The blue devil looked as if it were covered in blue flames as it hopped about the hayloft.

In addition, as we noted in an earlier chapter, the black blobs at times would sit at the bedsides of the human occupants of a home so frequently they were misidentified as the family dog; only when looked at directly would they reveal themselves.

Sadly, all the structures visited by the black blobs and the blue devil have been lost over the years to changes in land ownership. Luckily the children and grandchildren of locals have preserved the local verbal history.

Another area of interest in Whiteley Township is Mason Ridge Road, currently marked as part of the Warrior Trail. A tall, lanky specter is seen from time to time walking down the road dressed in mid- to late 1800s attire. Some of the witnesses compared his clothing and stature to Abraham Lincoln as he is reportedly tall and slender.

One witness recounted visiting an area of Mason Ridge Road with a group of students from Waynesburg College (now University) who were interested in conducting a ceremony in a small cemetery on private property. The witness, a local, served as a guide to the location as the college students were not from the immediate area. The witness

Mason Ridge Road. Credit: Kevin Paul.

stated that the students followed some written instructions for a ritual to raise the dead. Neither the students nor the witness believed it possible but when the ritual commenced a wispy, transparent figure of a person rose from the ground like some kind of terrifying mist. At that point both the witness and the college students ran for their cars and beat a hasty retreat.

Another individual played on the Warrior Trail with her sister as a child. Their activity attracted some kind of scenes from the past. First they clearly saw a small group of saddled, riderless horses. Soon after they stared in disbelief as Native Americans, all males, materialized slowly in front of them. The Native Americans seemed real enough but never acknowledged the presence of the two children. They walked for a distance, and then along with the horses faded slowly from sight. The siblings and others reported hearing the singing and drumming of the Native Americans at night.

Warrior Trail. Credit: Kevin Paul.

Without a doubt the most interesting report from the Kirby area involves a bachelor party cut short by the paranormal. According to reports published in the Waynesburg University *Yellow Jacket,* the fianceé of a young man living in the Morgantown, West Virginia area was a native of Greene County. Her grandfather had told her repeatedly that the Warrior Trail was haunted, an evil place to be avoided. That didn't stop the young woman from asking to hear about the hauntings, but repeated requests were denied. Once he even admonished her, "Not even God would touch that place."

As their wedding day approached, the bridegroom and some of his closest associates decided to embark upon a bachelor party/camping trip into Greene County. None of the young men were locals with any knowledge of the Warrior Trail or of the fact that their party/camp site was within 100 yards of the trail. To the best of their knowledge they had chosen an open field on top of a hill, nothing more.

Their reality changed with the coming of nightfall when the wind stopped and became silent. The blackish-gray sky turned blood red, and the entire field began to glow. A small bush was illuminated in blue and glowing white forms began to appear seemingly everywhere. The men saw dozens of figures, some Native Americans and some in full Civil War uniform.

At this point the fight or flight instinct was in full force, with flight prevailing. They hurriedly drove their car to the field entrance where a phantom soldier sat on one side of the entrance and a phantom Native American on the other. Once they made it to the roadway, the driver held his foot to the floor. A sharp left turn gave one young man a perfect view of a Native American running toward them and throwing a spear. Not sparing the horsepower, the carload of shaken young men sped back to Morgantown.

Five days passed. Gathering their wits about them, the young men decided to return to the field during daylight hours with their girlfriends. It was assumed that they would have nothing to fear during the day. They easily found their tire tracks in the field as the only evidence of their hastily abandoned campsite. Upon leaving the field, they turned toward Kirby and were promptly halted by a flat tire. Piling out to investigate, they were shocked to see an arrowhead in their tire.

Perhaps the young woman's grandfather was correct in his warnings about the Warrior Trail.

In August of 2013, a man was walking along the Warrior Trail in the general vicinity of Claughton Chapel Methodist Church. I have known this individual for most of my adult life and he is an established businessman in Waynesburg with strong ties to the community. This person was taking a short stroll on the Warrior Trail for the simple reason he had never done it before and on this particular day he had the time.

Parking near Claughton Chapel, he first walked east in the direction of Mason Ridge Road, and then turned westward to return to his car. Lost in his thoughts and enjoying the songbirds, he was frequently reminded that a construction crew was busy above ground at the nearby Cumberland Mine. Now and then he could make out the voices of the crew but there was no mistaking the sound of a sledgehammer striking steel beams as the men struggled to erect a structure. He paused when within sight of Claughton Chapel to enjoy the beauty of the summer afternoon when he noticed unusual sounds in the distance.

As the crew worked on the mine building, something would echo the sound of the sledgehammer striking steel. Each time the steel was struck, there was a corresponding knocking sound as if someone were beating on a piece of wood. If the sledgehammer struck three times, three knocks responded. The knocks also seemed to grow louder as if getting closer. As construction work continued, so did the knocking. Soon it was supplemented and then replaced by a whooping sound identical in number to the blows struck by the sledgehammer.

Puzzled at first, my friend stood and listened to determine what was knocking and making the whooping sound. It made no sense as it continued to draw near. Filled with a sudden uneasiness, he walked quickly to his car and left the area.

That night he struggled to understand what he had heard. Through the internet he contacted an ornithologist in neighboring Washington County who was at a loss to explain the whooping sound. One search led to another, eventually landing on links to Bigfoot sites featuring recorded vocalizations. Sure enough, what he had heard was very much like whooping calls and knocking sounds recorded by cryptozoologists in attempts to document the existence of Bigfoot.

Whether he heard Sasquatch remains to be seen, but it is interesting to note that his experience took place within easy walking distance of the area where the Mason Ridge specters have been seen. Unexplained lights, black blobs and blue devils were sighted as well as ghostly images that presented themselves to multiple witnesses on the Warrior Trail.

CHAPTER 13

THE CURIOUS CASE OF ART HUCK

Whiteley Township, like neighboring Franklin has been no stranger to the murderous mayhem so prevalent in local history. Case in point would be the adventures of one Mrs. Experience Bozarth, who in 1779 lived somewhere in Whiteley Township and according to accounts was "a lone woman." Whether she was abandoned, widowed or her husband was out of the area at her time of crisis is unclear. Experience's home was in a small cluster of cabins of which there were perhaps four in total. The exact location remains a mystery. For reasons unknown, in times of alarm neighbors would gather at Experience's cabin either because it offered the most shelter or because of her reputation of being "a fearless creature," or both.

In mid-March 1779, Native Americans were taking aggressive action toward the settlers of Greene County, and as was their custom Experience's neighbors all gathered at her cabin in response to the news of unrest. A few days' wait brought no attack, and the group began to relax and disperse. Only two men remained at the cabin with Experience and several children of neighboring families. It was at that moment the Indians struck, shooting one man in the chest as he attempted to exit the cabin in defense of the group. The force of the bullet dropped him to the floor, and the warrior who shot him darted into the house and attacked the remaining man while others were "slaughtering children in the yard."

The remaining man tossed the attacking warrior onto a bed and called to Experience for a knife with which to kill his attacker and was shot dead for his effort. Experience immediately attacked the warrior with an axe and disemboweled him on the spot. His screams in turn caused the remainder of the war party engaged in killing children to enter the cabin to aid their comrade.

The first warrior who looked through the still open doorway was welcomed by the axe-wielding Experience, who promptly split his skull having "cleft it in twain by a murderous stroke." Over the next few days repeated attacks were rebuffed by the remaining settlers until a relief party arrived and drove the Native Americans away.

It was in these hills and valleys of Whiteley and Franklin Townships that a modern-day adventurer of sorts appeared. I've known Art Huck (not his real name) for many years, and at first glance he appears to be Mr. Average: middle age, middle class, happily married with children. In every sense he's your everyday working man with one exception: he has a lifelong experience with the paranormal and unexplained.

The illuminated being

Art's first brush with the unexplained occurred when he was about seven years old. He was awakened after midnight one evening by what he has described as a man made entirely of light. The figure stood about six feet tall and was perfectly still, arms at its sides much like the anatomical figures one sees on a doctor's office wall. The palms faced outward, and no discernable facial features were visible. Art was never sure if the figure's feet were touching the floor or if it were suspended in mid-air. It made no sound whatsoever, nor attempted to communicate in any way that Art was aware of. It seemed only to be interested in showing itself and watching him.

The figure not only generated a considerable amount of light but also was illuminated from behind. Art compared its brightness to that of looking into oncoming car headlights at night: bright, but he could still make out the details of the part of the room in which the figure appeared. Nothing seemed to be out of place except for the light being, which stood perhaps 10 feet from Art's bed. The light from behind the entity looked almost like an aura. It seemed to come from a central point behind the figure and radiate outward in a circle. The figure was much brighter, almost white, when compared to the more yellow background lighting. Despite its intensity the light did not illuminate the entire room which Art shared with his younger sibling. The entity appeared to be solid, as Art could not see through it to the source of the aura light, which seemed to be centered behind the being. Art has said he believed the entity was standing in front of some kind of doorway, but to this day he has no inkling what was on the other side.

When the figure faded, Art very dutifully and immediately reported the sighting to his parents, who assured him that he had been dreaming and it was all a figment of his imagination. Nevertheless, for the remainder of the time he slept in that room, he was uncomfortable being near the corner where the being and doorway appeared. This feeling continued throughout his high school years and even during college when he returned home on weekends, summer break or holidays.

Early paranormal schooling

Art's grandmother was a different story, however, and while to his recollection she never commented one way or another on his encounter with the man of light, she was dedicated to providing him with a mixture of Appalachian folklore and the Gospel. She was equally at home discussing the Bible, the life of Jesus Christ, working by the signs of the moon, and how to forecast the weather through observation of nature. She also subscribed to a weekly newspaper that at the time carried a variety of stories, including the paranormal. It was on her sun porch that Art first read of the Hopkinsville, Kentucky Goblins Case from 1955 in which seven members of a family were terrorized by unknown creatures who dropped down from the sky in a craft. Family members ran for their lives when gunfire had no effect upon the unwelcome visitors. Art was excited by the story and showed it to his grandmother, whose only reply was, "Well, those fellows were shooting at something, weren't they?"

Art's grandparents lived in what was at that time a rural portion of Franklin Township and within an easy bicycle ride of his home. They owned a small farm and had the traditional assortment of livestock one would find in southwestern Pennsylvania during the 1950s and 1960s: cattle, sheep, chickens and an occasional pig. While by today's standards neither was educated, both were very capable and well versed in farm life and its challenges.

Every winter Art's grandfather would bring his flock of sheep into the barn at lambing time. For the farmer, lambing is a crucial time when profit is made or lost. A good lambing year means an abundance of healthy lambs that will go to market for a return on the investment of time and money placed into them. A bad lambing year, whether it is due to predators, bad weather, difficult births or a poor nurturing from the ewes, will yield little or reduced income for the farmer. Thus, Art's grandfather, like careful shepherds everywhere, did the most he could to safeguard the sheep during lambing.

Sheep seemed like peculiar animals to Art when he helped on his grandparents' farm. Sometimes, not often, they would be found dead in the fields. Finding a dead sheep now and then was of no surprise to his grandfather, nor was it unusual for seemingly healthy lambs to die unexpectedly. Such is life on the farm. However, the lambing season of 1961 proved to be a challenging one for a different reason.

Mutilated lamb deaths

Art's grandfather had brought the entire flock into the safety of the barn nearest the house to allow for close monitoring of lambing. It was in the dead of winter, and they had a good start on what appeared to be a trouble-free lambing season. The sheep were penned inside the barn, fed and watered daily, and the lambs were healthy and strong. It was nearly time to open the latched door and let the sheep and lambs outside when the problems started.

His grandfather began finding dead lambs, usually one per night, with a peculiar wound to the top of their heads. Each was found with a hole about the size of a pencil in the top of their heads as if someone had taken the time and effort to drill a hole. There was no blood loss, no noises or sounds at night and the family dogs did not take notice of anything unusual. They were killed one per night. Each had the hole drilled neatly into the top of its head, and six were found in that condition. Although they were familiar with wounds found on livestock and chickens caused by dogs, foxes, weasels and other common predators they had never seen wounds such as these. Consultations with their friends and neighbors on what may have caused them were fruitless and the curious events may have been forgotten were it not for more peculiar events yet to come.

A creepy green glow and mystery lights

As the years passed, Art spent as much time as possible on the farm. He liked the country lifestyle and it afforded him the opportunity to do things many of his peers could not: driving before age 16, walking in the woods, target shooting and listening to his grandfather's friends tell stories. He became friends with two brothers who lived on the opposite side of the hill.

One Friday during the summer of 1970, Art and his two friends decided to go camping. This was a regular occurrence, and they laid out their campsite on a portion of what is now the state game lands along

Temple Ridge in Whiteley Township. It was a considerable hike from his friends' house to the campsite, but one they had made easily on several occasions.

Their gear consisted of sleeping bags, matches, food, water and flashlights. They also equipped themselves with two miner's lights, which consisted of a battery pack worn around the waist connected by an electrical cord to a light that could be hand-held or attached to a hat. The three set out late in the day and were looking forward to another night of watching for meteors and poking the campfire.

Part of the appeal to camping on Temple Ridge was the warning they received from an elderly gentleman who lived near the area that it was a dangerous place to be. Depending on the day, he would assure them with a twinkle in his eye that the ridge was a favorite hunting ground for a pack of wild dogs, that it was haunted, or that a man who lived in a small house along Temple Ridge Road had committed suicide by hanging himself in a tree near their campsite.

The boys always assumed the warnings were tongue-in-cheek, but on more than one occasion they did see a strange greenish glow in the pasture where they camped. Always assuming it to be foxfire (a type of bioluminescence caused by fungi), the three young men usually ignored it.

One evening it was very close to their campfire, and upon investigation they found it to be a collection of pale green-glowing dots moving back and forth along the stems of grasses and plants in the field.

As the night wore on and the fire began to fade, the three stretched out on the ground in their sleeping bags. Spotting meteors was a popular pasttime for them, and this night was no exception. The dark sky was not competing with artificial light, and soon satellites and meteors were visible.

As they lay gazing skyward they soon noticed that some of the satellites were turning at right angles. There they were, crossing the sky high above the earth and then suddenly objects would make 90-degree turns without slowing down and move off in another direction. Art and the older brother were fascinated by the events and speculated about what they had seen until they fell asleep, but the younger brother was terrified and was awake all night. At dawn they hiked homeward for breakfast.

Soon the trio decided to make a return trip to their Temple Ridge campground. They loaded up their gear, flashlights and freshly recharged miner's lights, and set out on foot at dusk. This time was a little different than the others in that they began to experience problems with their trusted lights. Between the three of them they carried a total of five battery-powered lights: two miner's lights and three multi-cell flashlights. These lights had proven reliable time and again during forays into the night, both on and off of Temple Ridge. All three were quite familiar with their operation and changed or charged the batteries frequently.

On this evening, the farther out Temple Ridge Road they walked, the dimmer the lights became. First one, then another, and another grew dim and went out, until all five were completely dead and useless. A debate among Art and his friends quickly sprang up: Art and the older brother wanted to continue but the youngest, still fearful from the expedition two weeks earlier, lobbied to return home. His pleas became desperate and soon were laced with tears, forcing the older two to agree to return home.

As they reversed course and made their way homeward and off Temple Ridge, one by one all five of the lights began to work again. Once back at his friends' house, Art and the older brother checked the lights and confirmed that all had fresh batteries or had been recharged earlier in the day when the decision to camp had been made. The failure of the lights combined with the creeping green glow in the pasture of the previous trip marked the end of the Temple Ridge campground.

The invisible tracker

Soon after, Art settled into his high school career which was full of the usual misadventures for young men coming of age in the late 1960s and early 1970s. His high school years were not extraordinary although he had a large group of friends he managed to spend time with on weekends and after school. Temple Ridge Road continued to be of interest to him as it was a well-known, well used lover's lane. Many weekend evenings would find Art and his date for the evening in a parked car not far from the old campground.

It was long after his high school days when Art learned from topographic maps that the old campground and favorite date destination were but a stone's throw from a long-abandoned cemetery. During this time the local newspaper carried sightings of Bigfoot in parts of Greene County. These stories delighted Art and his friends, and many an evening was spent cruising the back roads searching for Sasquatch, which they referred to as Red Eyes based on rumors heard at the time. While amusing to him at the time, years later Art heard a lecture by Bigfoot researcher Stan Gordon, who has documented the incredible number of Bigfoot and UFO sightings in the southwestern Pennsylvania area at that time.

After high school graduation Art picked up extra part-time income working on three area farms. Chores at one would see him returning to Temple Ridge operating farm machinery by day and at times by night. In May of 1974 Art was operating farm equipment in a field on Temple Ridge when the tractor became stuck in a ditch. Operator error was the cause, and Art was angry with himself as he worked for nearly an hour to free the stubbornly stuck machine. Realizing he would require help, he set off on foot toward a side road that offered the quickest route to the homestead of the farmer who had employed him, and the assistance he needed to free the equipment.

As he walked his anger faded, and he settled in to maintaining a brisk pace to get help as quickly as possible. He turned off of Temple Ridge Road, walked about 100 yards to an area that was wooded on both sides of the road, and heard the sound of footsteps paralleling him in the trees. They did not sound like an animal but more like a man – a very large man, pacing him just out of sight in the brush. When Art walked, he heard footsteps; when he stopped, the other footsteps stopped as well.

Art called out to his shy companion, who refused to answer or identify himself but made certain Art heard him shuffling through the trees and leaves. The footsteps were unmistakable, and heavy. Annoyed at first, Art suddenly developed a sense of being watched by something that may not have his best interest in mind. It was bipedal, and very large. Like the fading flashlights of his recent past, Art did not realize at the time that these footsteps are classic signs of encountering the paranormal. He did have one fleeting and frightening thought: perhaps it was Bigfoot. Suddenly, searching for Red Eyes wasn't so entertaining.

Art was thankful to see an approaching pickup truck which he flagged down and hitched a ride with back to the farm. Within two hours Art and the man who hired him had retrieved the equipment with no harm done. Seeing no sign of anything unusual, Art did not mention the footsteps he heard so clearly.

Encounter with a landed craft

On the following summer solstice, June 21, 1974, Art was once again earning a few extra dollars filling in for the same farmer who was out of town. Back on Temple Ridge operating farm machinery, Art again had difficulty, only this time it was mechanical. A chain broke and luckily Art had the means to repair it on site. It was late in the day, and dark by the time Art was completing some of his fieldwork. It was well after sunset and the field where he was working was lit only by the lights of the tractor he was operating. Art was literally a stone's throw from where he had heard the footsteps the month before when he encountered something that caused him to stop the machine in its tracks.

Ahead of Art and sitting on the ground was a bright light, which Art immediately suspected to be the tail lights of a car parked in the field. Temple Ridge was still a well-known lovers' lane and it was not at all uncommon to find young couples entwined behind steamy windows on a warm summer evening. Art quickly realized that this was unlike any car he had seen, however, and the design of the lights was unfamiliar to him. It was still some distance from him when he halted the tractor and killed both the lights and the engine to study the vehicle undetected by its occupants.

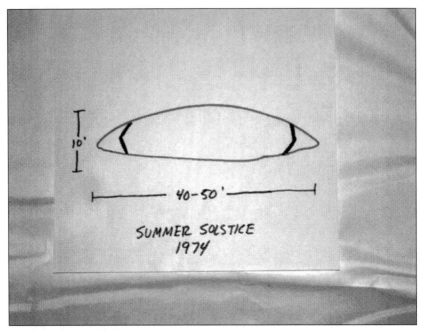

Landed UFO on Temple Ridge, June 21, 1974. Credit: Art Huck.

As he sat in the darkness, Art began to realize there was something unusual about the light in the field. First was the color, a bright red-orange like that of molten metal instead of the duller red of an automobile's lights. Second was the shape, flat on the bottom with a rounded top which tapered to a point at each end and culminated in defined arrowhead-like features.

He was puzzled by this as it in no way resembled a motor vehicle of the time; in fact, it looked more like a flat-bottomed cigar with rounded top and pointed ends. Finally, was the size of the object: it was immense, the size of a tractor-trailer; easily over 40 feet long and 10 to 12 feet high.

Art sat on the tractor, immobilized by his confusion and curiosity. Suddenly he panicked, for he realized he was staring at something that shouldn't be there, was of unknown origin, and was much too close for comfort. Fearing an encounter with extraterrestrials, he frantically tried to start the tractor to leave the area immediately. After several attempts and with some difficulty, the machine finally clattered into life. He threw caution to the wind as he pushed the tractor for every available ounce of power and speed he could coax from it to leave the area as rapidly as possible.

When he returned to the farmstead he shut down the machine and without hesitation jumped into his car and sped home. Sleep was fitful that night as he wrestled with the images of what he had seen. What was sitting in the field that so defied description? Art kept coming to the same chilling conclusion: he had witnessed a UFO sitting upon the ground.

The next morning, he returned to the farm once again, determined to put the event behind him. Whatever he had seen he would eventually understand, he reasoned, and he decided to return to the spot at the end of the workday in an attempt to put the event behind him.

That night he did just that. He parked his car along Temple Ridge Road and walked into the same field at the same time of night. Everything was as it should be: the stars were overhead, the field was dark, and the night air was filled with the sounds of nocturnal insects and an occasional bat. The object was gone.

Seeing nothing out of the ordinary, Art laughed at himself and decided the entire event was a figment of his imagination. He was too tired, had been in the hot sun too long, or had gone too long without a meal, for one simply did not see large cigar-shaped glowing objects sitting in the fields of Whiteley Township. It just didn't happen.

Art returned to his car, still chuckling as he turned around to go home. He elected to travel Temple Ridge Road as it was a shorter distance to drive, the cooler air of evening filling the vehicle courtesy of the rolled down windows.

He had traveled less than 500 feet when a large bird swooped down in front of the car. Illuminated by the headlights, it was 10 to 15 feet in front of the vehicle, matching its speed perfectly and maintaining its lead. Light gray in color, it had a tremendous wingspan that stretched from one side of the road to the other. Barely moving its wings, it glided as much as flew just a few feet above the road surface and exactly in dead center of the road.

The panic of the previous night returned as Art drove on, staring in disbelief at the giant bird with thin wings, a tubular tapered body, and what resembled the head of an owl. The rationalization of the previous

Approximate location on Temple Ridge Road where Art Huck had his giant winged creature sighting. Credit: Art Huck.

night's encounter melted away, and mentally Art acknowledged that he had in fact encountered something foreign to his reality. The moment he admitted to himself the reality of his earlier sighting the winged creature banked away, never gaining altitude and vanishing among the trees. From that moment on, Art believed.

It is interesting to note the recurring theme of owls appearing in conjunction with UFOs, reports of extraterrestrials, and even alleged alien abductions. Researchers Nick Redfern, Mike Clelland, Whitney Streiber and others have all delved into the possibility that sightings of what appear to be impossibly large owls could in fact be encounters with extraterrestrials, especially those who abduct humans. Many abductees tell stories of encountering very large owls or sighting many owls in unusual places. It is the researchers' conjecture that what abductees are recognizing as owls are in fact screen (false) memories placed there by their alien captors to camouflage their work and movement among us.

Are some of us "hard-wired" to have more extraordinary experiences than the average person? Many researchers say this is a marked pattern. While most, if not all, of us will see a ghost or a cryptid or a UFO at some point in life, an unknown percentage of the human race lives with one foot in the doorway to the unknown. Perhaps Art is one of those adventurers.

CHAPTER 14

UFOs Over Greene County

Every year, several thousand UFOs seen in Pennsylvania are reported to researchers, UFO-related organizations, and the media. Undoubtedly thousands more go unreported. Greene County is not the most UFO-active in the state – Allegheny County holds that record – but it has a history of activity going back to the mid-20th century. Craft of all sizes and shapes are reported, the most common being round saucers; cigars; triangles; and rectangular boxes. Many of them sport flashing lights of varying colors.

In 1950 or 1951, Donald "Shorty" Waychoff and his brother, Bob, were at their family home in Wayne Township. A cow pasture was adjacent to the house. Bob went outside one afternoon, leaving Shorty inside, and was astonished to see a huge saucer-shaped craft hovering low over the pasture, about 100 yards away. It was rotating and had flashing multi-colored lights on its rim. Bob shouted for Shorty to come outside, but no sooner than Shorty had left the front door, the craft was gone. Bob witnessed it shoot straight up into the sky and vanish.

On into the 1960s, numerous other residents periodically saw a huge saucer-shaped craft rimmed with flashing lights of different colors. Many of these sightings, too, were during the day. Concurrent with the UFOs were huge luminous crosses seen in the nighttime sky.

Numerous unidentified flying objects have been reported to fly the friendly skies of Franklin Township as well. In the late 1950s, a group of children were enjoying a June afternoon on a hilltop just outside of Waynesburg. One noticed an enormous silver saucer-shaped object hovering nearby. The group watched it for nearly a half hour and were astonished to see two smaller discs approximately 300 feet long emerge from the much larger object. All three craft were of the same general shape. The witnesses reported that the larger object left the area at an extreme rate of speed, so fast that one reported that it crossed the sky in the amount of time it took to turn his head.

One Sunday afternoon in August of 1979, a Pennsylvania State Police helicopter with a crew of two were flying south at 2000 feet just outside of Waynesburg. At 4:05 PM the two troopers were astonished to see a round object that was silvery blue in color flying in the opposite direction at a leisurely pace. The two officers estimated its size to be two feet around and 10 inches thick. The object was on course to pass within 50 feet of the helicopter when it began to accelerate. It made a loud whooshing sound and sped past the aircraft. The helicopter was traveling at 120 mph, but when the pilot turned to pursue the object it had already flown out of sight.

During July 1986, two teenage girls were under the watchful eye of their adult babysitter at sunset near Waynesburg. The girls saw three orange UFOs to the east that were perhaps four to five miles from their location. The objects flew in a horizontal formation, in line with each other. After a few moments they sped off to the north. Within a few minutes two military helicopters flew overhead at low altitude headed toward the area where the orange objects were first seen.

In May of 2012 witnesses traveling on Interstate 79 near Waynesburg saw a bright light that seemed to be surrounded by a group of six jets. The light suddenly vanished, but the jets lingered in the area and eventually flew off. During November a huge elongated object covered with lights was spotted hovering over trees near the highway close to Waynesburg.

In 2013 a couple witnessed several UFOs during October and November in the vicinity of Waynesburg. The first sightings were of white objects that had colored lights on them, but in November they witnessed through binoculars a cigar-shaped object covered in white pulsating light from top to bottom. The object then took on a rectangular shape and was gliding along at a low altitude but faster than jet aircraft.

There continued to be sightings as 2014 was a busy year for UFOs over Franklin Township. A large diamond-shaped light pulsating green, red and blue rotated as it hovered near Waynesburg. Another witness reported a large fireball crossing the sky. It suddenly stopped, began zig-zagging, and then vanished. Another person reported a flashing blue-white light moving rapidly across the sky, stopping suddenly, hovering, and then zooming off at a 45-degree angle. The witness expressed surprise at how the object could stop so quickly and remain in the air.

Perhaps residents should all keep their eyes on the skies.

Black rectangles

In early December 2015, Fred (not his real name) was driving from Waynesburg east toward Uniontown where he was to work that day. Fred had been employed for a number of years as a contractor and traveled several days a week into Fayette County to his job site. In fact, Fred had made the trip so many times in all types of weather, day and night, that he was quite familiar with the route, and often stated he could drive it blindfolded. The daily commute had become routine and never changing, so much so that it was almost boring.

On the morning of December 3, 2015, Fred encountered something quite extraordinary that grabbed his attention, as told in his own words:

At approximately 6:30 I was eastbound on 21 and about to pass the now closed Hatfield Ferry power station. There's a slight hill above the river, and once you crest that you have a clear view of the bridge and far side of the Monongahela River. This morning there was what initially appeared to be an aircraft flying west with its landing lights on. I say flying west because I was assuming I was looking at an airliner as the two white lights were just about the right distance apart to be landing lights. This was very much out of the ordinary because there is nowhere directly west of Hatfield for a jet to land close enough that it would be in approach, descending with the landing lights on. From where I was on the Greene County side of the river, the aircraft's apparent wingspan, based upon the distance between the landing lights, indicated a plane too large for either Greene County or the Morgantown airports.

I've noticed many aircraft during my morning commutes at low altitude, and they always have visible strobes and navigation lights. This had neither, which was odd considering its size. As I crossed the bridge into Fayette County and began climbing the hill at perhaps 50 mph, I was able to get a much better look at the object in the air just south of 21, literally above and beside the road.

I slowed and got a clear look at the thing. My (contractor's) job requires us to guess distances and lengths sometimes, and my best guess is it was maybe 300 feet off the ground, 120 feet or so in length, and rectangular. It was, for lack of a better description, the shape of a Lincoln log without the notches on the ends. I would estimate it to be 15 feet in height and width, square on the ends. On the surface facing westward were two very large round lights, evenly spaced, about the color of incandescent light bulbs. In the middle was a bright blue-white light, almost a pin point compared to the other two, and the color of an indoor LED light. As I said, there were no wings, no rotors, no strobes, no navigation lights. It was black as coal against the sky and rectangular. I was so stunned it never occurred to me to stop and try and get a picture with my phone. It was so close to the road I nearly passed directly underneath it.

I spent most of the day feeling like I had been punched in the stomach, and truthfully was a little anxious on the drive home, and for several days afterward.

Researcher Stan Gordon received a report of another rectangular object over Fayette County. On October 16, 2016 a couple was driving Route 43 in Fayette County and saw a misty cloud of black smoke as they approached the crest of a hill. It was above a group of trees and began to take the shape of a large black rectangular object. It took up a position over the southbound lanes, only to quickly move over to the northbound side on which they were driving. As the object cleared the northbound lanes it stopped and formed a circular shape that did not appear as solid as the rectangle. It then very quickly took the shape of a rectangle, moved back over the southbound lanes and suddenly vanished from sight.

Triangular craft

In the late 20th and early 21st centuries, triangular-shaped UFOs made their appearances around the world. These craft are usually black, sometimes with pulsating colored lights at the points of the triangle or on the underside. They are large and silent, and hover or slowly cruise at low altitudes over cities and highways. Sightings usually take place at night. The craft are usually visible to radar.

One of the most famous waves of black triangle sightings occurred over a several-year period in the mid-1980s in the Hudson River Valley region of New York State. The craft were witnessed by thousands of people.

Another famous wave occurred in Belgium from 1989-1990. During these incidents, Belgian fighter aircraft attempted to intercept the objects (getting a successful missile lock at two occasions) only to be outmaneuvered.

At about the same time authorities in the United Kingdom launched an investigation known as Project Condign, which examined UFO reports and included triangular UFOs. A key conclusion of the report was that no attempt should be made on the part of civilian or RAF Air Defense aircraft to outmaneuver these objects except to place them astern to mitigate the risk of collision.

Many have theorized that triangular UFO sightings are in reality black budget US Air Force projects such as the alleged Aurora, the Lockheed-Martin Blackstar, or the TR-3 Black Manta.

We will mention a black triangle case from Virginia because of the similarity it had to a sighting in Greene County. Pennsylvania-based researcher Stan Gordon shared this report dated May 30, 2013 from Hiwassee, Virginia concerning a triangular UFO sighted the previous day. Around 10 that evening, a man was driving east in a heavy-duty pickup truck when he noticed three lights in a triangular pattern at about 300 feet in altitude.

Stopping his vehicle, he observed the object and noticed one light on top and two on the bottom. He described them as "white, like porcelain" and that the light was not reflective, and the object made no sound.

The witness lowered his window to obtain a photograph with his new cellphone, but the device malfunctioned and displayed a black screen. Three times he attempted to take a picture. Each time as he leaned out of the window his phone display would go black, and each time he returned the phone functioned normally.

After observing the object for about three minutes, he saw it shoot straight up into the air with a rumbling sound described as louder than the Concorde jet. The witness stated that he also felt the sound in the pit of his stomach, and that his truck shook as well.

After regaining his composure, the man drove away – only to see an object in the rear-view mirror. Stopping the truck, he got out to better view the object which he described as similar, although he could not say for certain it was not a different craft. After about 30 seconds the object sped off to the north and out of sight.

Triangular craft in Greene County

In Pennsylvania, there have been more than 10,000 black triangle sightings, and Greene County and the surrounding area have had their share.

In 2013, a witness and her husband watched a flying triangle with the signature pulsating lights move over Waynesburg from 10 PM until 1 AM one September evening. They saw what appeared to be the same object accompanied by several smaller ones a month later. In each case the craft was described as either a triangle or an upside down "V."

Shortly thereafter, three men were patronizing a popular Waynesburg business when one exited the building to drive home. As he neared his vehicle he was gripped by an irresistible urge to look skyward. Shifting his gaze upward, he was stunned to see what he described as an immense black triangular craft hovering about 300 feet in the air. He was astounded and moved quickly inside the building to tell the other two men, who went outside and also witnessed the craft. From their vantage point the trio could see only one bright light on the belly of the unidentified craft. It hovered for a time, and then shot straight up until it was out of sight.

In March 2016 several witnesses in Mather and Jefferson reported seeing a large triangular craft moving slowly at low altitude. Like the craft reported in Hiwassee, Virginia, this hovering vehicle sounded like an extremely large jet. According to one witness it appeared around 10 PM on March 2 and moved very slowly down the entire length of her home. She rushed from one window to another to get a better look at the craft when suddenly it shot straight up into the air. It was extremely loud and reminded the witness of a Space Shuttle launch she had seen; the sound shook her entire house. The witness, like the one in Virginia, described the sound as similar to a jet engine, only much louder.

Another member of her family was outside during the event and described the craft as being somewhat like the B-2 Stealth bomber but without any navigational lights. About a half-hour later the same craft was sighted a few miles away and then in several locations around Greene County the next day. A similar object was also sighted over nearby California, Pennsylvania.

Two witnesses reported seeing a triangular object hovering at about 300 feet in early November 2016 while traveling on Route 188 near Waynesburg. As they were driving around 5:19 in the afternoon of the 10th, they were forced to reduce speed to safely follow a large truck. A bright reflection caught the attention of the driver, who noticed what she thought was a helicopter hovering a few hundred feet in the air. Given the slow pace of traffic due to the large truck they were following, she could divert her attention periodically to the object in the sky.

Upon closer examination, the witnesses realized that the craft was not a helicopter but was in fact a three-dimensional flying triangle. The bright light that caught their attention seemed to be reflected sunlight from a very shiny surface, and that it was on the left side of the craft. The vehicle had no visible wings, engines, rotors or propellers, nor did it display any noticeable navigation lights. The witnesses also reported that their car radio temporarily quit playing, and during the time the object was in sight all they could hear was static.

About 45 minutes later an emergency room physician and his wife reported seeing a similar object in Washington, Pennsylvania and observed it for nearly an hour. They reported witnessing multiple aircraft circling the object, and during the event cellphone service was disrupted. The object suddenly vanished, and cellphone service returned to normal.

Cloud UFOs

One type of UFO reported every now and then is the "cloud UFO" – a light or craft seen within an illuminated cloud. In fact, some believe that UFOs disguise themselves as certain kinds of clouds.

One night in 2011, a young man and two of his friends saw bright white orb-like lights inside clouds that followed them as they traveled through the county.

Doug (not his real name) was out driving with his girlfriend near Bobtown, heading east toward the home of the mother of one of their friends. Looking up, they saw an illuminated cloud that contained three bright white lights that seemed to be connected to each other in a rough circle. The lights rotated within the cloud. They observed the phenomenon for several minutes.

Turning in a southward direction, they again saw the same thing in a different cloud in a different part of the sky.

When they arrived at their destination to meet their friend, they all went out into the back yard to skywatch – and again saw the three white lights inside yet another cloud. Other individuals in the Bobtown area have reported seeing white lights as well when out for an evening stroll or sitting on their deck.

Doug's encounters with the cloud UFOs are not limited to Greene County. A number of years ago he was walking through a crowd in Pittsburgh with friends waiting to see a movie. He gazed skyward, only to once again see cloud UFOs overhead. He was amazed, not at the UFOs, but at the passersby who were missing something truly extraordinary simply because they were not observing their environment.

Other experiencers report the same circumstances – they have a sighting while others around them do not or are not even interested in looking up. Perhaps some of us are "tuned" to certain kinds of experiences more than others.

CHAPTER 15

NIGHT HOWLERS AND FOREST PROWLERS

Nearly every portion of the rural United States that is wooded and somewhat remote plays host to one of the mainstays of campfire storytelling and indigenous peoples all over the planet: Bigfoot, aka Sasquatch. These large and lumbering entities have been seen by people from all walks of life for as long as individuals have had either the curiosity or fortitude to venture off underneath the forest canopy or down the seldom used trail. More recently, it seems all that is required to experience a Bigfoot encounter is merely to go for a drive in the country.

Greene County is no exception to an occasional visit by what is generally described as a seven or eight-foot-tall bipedal creature covered with brown shaggy hair. Sometimes our local Sasquatches have a terrible odor similar to rotten eggs or sulfur, and some witnesses report the trademark red eyes peering at them as reflected in their headlights or flashlight beam. Sasquatch, whatever it may be, has been sighted all over the county, ranging from near the hospital in Waynesburg to deep in the state game lands near the West Virginia state line.

One encounter took place during 1969 in the southeastern Greene County community of Greensboro. A group of youths were attempting to take a clandestine swim at the local park after hours one hot summer evening. The cool water of the park pool would be made even more enjoyable by sneaking in while the facility was closed, thus avoiding the expense of paid admission. Their mission was going as planned when, much to their chagrin, the park manager who lived on the park grounds realized there were unauthorized and unsupervised kids attempting to use the swimming pool. When challenged by the park manager, the youths immediately scattered to all points of the compass and in great haste so as not to be caught by the manager.

One young man headed for the railroad tracks that ran alongside the Monongahela River, which provided an escape route that was easy to follow in the darkness. The young man was making his best possible speed along the tracks when he ran into what may first have seemed to be a foul-smelling, large, hairy tree. Blocking his retreat was none other than Sasquatch. Bouncing off the creature, the young man lay on his back looking up at what must have seemed to be unthinkable. Jumping to his feet, he scurried away, telling his friends of what he had encountered.

Throughout the early 1970s there were a series of Sasquatch sightings that I recall quite well. At the time I was attending Waynesburg Central High School and from time to time we would pile into our parents' cars and venture off into the night via the narrow and sometimes seldom traveled secondary roads searching for what we called Red Eyes. More often than not, these expeditions to discover the secrets of paranormal prowlers were an excuse to be alone with female companions whose emotional and physical well-being had far more to fear from the young men piloting the vehicles in which they were riding than from any chance encounter with Bigfoot.

During that time Pennsylvania was experiencing a great number of UFO sightings, and in the case of western Pennsylvania, Bigfoot sightings as well. There were documented reports out of nearby Fayette County of strange creatures, UFOs, and of a man who acted strangely after an encounter. These only served to whet our appetite for adventures into the unknown, and we sped off into the darkness in search of the unexplained. We never stopped to consider what we would do should we find it.

Many of our quests for Sasquatch took us in the general direction of Jefferson and Carmichaels. We graduated in 1974, thus ending our searches. It was truly a case of being in the right place but the wrong time.

In September 1975 a hunter was target shooting with his bow near Stringtown in Cumberland Township when he realized he was being watched by a dark, muscular humanoid nearly eight feet in height. The creature slowly approached him, pausing between steps, and the hunter left the area. Returning later, he saw very large footprints, broken branches, and trampled grass in the area where he had seen Sasquatch.

In 1987, a man and his son were out in the state game lands of Jackson Township, western Greene County. Their goal that night was to see wildlife, notably raccoons, foxes and possibly even coyotes. As a lure, they played a recording of a rabbit in distress hoping the sound would attract other wildlife. The recording worked, perhaps too well. Expecting to hear the chatter of a raccoon or the yips of coyotes, they instead were greeted with a strange vocalization that was loud, deep-throated and low-pitched. In addition to be being unfamiliar to them, the vocalization seemed to have an angry tone to it.

The pair then heard something large approaching them and shined their light in the direction of the sound, only to be greeted by a pair of red-orange eyes staring back at them. They observed the creature for nearly 10 minutes and described it as very tall. It had no neck or nose and was covered with reddish brown hair. As the creature moved among the trees, the witnesses noted it easily broke off tree branches three to six inches in diameter that were five to six feet off the ground.

In 2004, an individual was walking near Nemacolin in Cumberland Township and reported seeing a creature that was eight feet in height that weighed an estimated 400 pounds and was accompanied by a foul odor. Another couple living near what was then Greene County Memorial Hospital in Franklin Township returned home from a dinner date only to discover a six-foot-tall creature visiting their fenced-in garden. To discourage deer and other animals, the garden was surrounded by a six-foot-tall chain link fence topped with barb wire. They described their visitor as covered in dark brown hair and resembling a large chimpanzee. It glanced briefly at them, then returned its attention to the tomatoes and zucchini it was sampling at its leisure.

From December 2007 to December 2008, several sightings were reported near the town of Clarksville. Two of the Bigfoot sightings were reported within 10 days of each other. The first encounter was between a group of boys and a very large creature with big hands and feet with dark skin and was a brownish red in color. They reported that it emitted a bad odor and howled loudly. Less than two weeks later two men driving in the general vicinity encountered a hairy creature that was seven to eight feet tall. This creature had a terrible odor and howled loudly as well. The following March another individual encountered a creature matching the same general description: brownish red and very large (estimated by witnesses to weigh 600-700 pounds). It howled loudly and smelled like rotten eggs.

The Night Howlers and Dark Walker

I can't take credit for the term "Night Howlers," but will attribute it to Regis (not his real name, now deceased), who lived not far from the Mason-Dixon line that separates Greene County from Monongalia County, West Virginia. Regis had lived in that area for many years and told a mutual friend about the Night Howlers that he claimed visited him on more than one occasion. The Night Howlers were often heard but never seen. They approached Regis' home from the wooded hills of West Virginia and serenaded him periodically with loud howls, screeches and hoarse wails. Regis eventually tired of the at times disturbing nocturnal

One of the Night Howlers. Credit: John Weaver

racket and began keeping a loaded rifle in his living room in case he should ever see one of the Night Howlers. He invited a friend to come hear the serenade several times, but the friend always declined, stating that the 30.06 rifle by the front door always worried him.

Regis was not the only person to have encountered Night Howlers. In 1946-47, John (not his real name), along with his mother and grandfather, had a series of encounters with some type of howling hominid near Aleppo. John and his mother moved in with her father – John's grandfather – following the death of John's father at an early age, as well as the passing of John's grandmother. Single mothers were not too common in the late 1940s. Since John's grandfather was alone as well, it made perfect sense for the three to live together in rural, remote western Greene County.

John's grandfather was a handyman of sorts and had a small blacksmith shop at his farm. The landscape near their home was partly wooded, and in the summer of 1946 the trio began hearing repeated howls emanating from the trees. The cries always occurred at night. The grandfather never seemed concerned by them; in fact, he and young John continued to supplement their diet by frequently hunting squirrels and other game in those same woods without ever witnessing or seeing any sign of an unusual animal lurking about.

During the spring of 1947, John was helping his grandfather in the blacksmith shop when he caught a glimpse of what he described as an ape-like creature standing at the edge of the woods. Alarmed, he called to his grandfather to come and see the creature. His grandfather very nonchalantly stood in the doorway of the blacksmith shop, smoking calmly as he watched the creature turn and disappear among the trees. John, still upset, told his mother of the sighting that evening, and she in turn confronted her father about what her son had seen.

He stated that he had never mentioned the presence of the creature he referred to as the Dark Walker, as he was afraid that his daughter would pack up her son and leave him there alone. The old man also stated that he had been told the Native Americans had encountered the creature and others like it as well and called them Stone Spirits. They not only considered them evil but that when seen someone would die. Grandfather went on to say that he considered them a harbinger of death as well, since his wife, John's grandmother, had passed away shortly after he had last encountered the Dark Walker.

The howling of the creature continued, and as the year progressed it seemed that it was coming closer and closer to the house. One evening as they sat on the porch listening to the radio, John's grandfather suddenly started looking out toward the barn and told John to bring him his handgun and some ammunition. Loading his Webley .455 revolver, he told John and his mother to stay in the house while he remained outside.

Soon after they heard three shots followed by bloodcurdling screams. Sudden silence followed the screams; then John and his mother heard the old man shout to them, instructing them to stay inside the house until he returned. They heard his pickup truck start. A short time later he drove slowly past the house allowing John and his mother to see what appeared to be something loaded in the back of the truck concealed beneath a tarp.

Given that there already had been considerable excitement that evening, John's mother marched him off to bed. The next morning John greeted his grandfather who was drinking his morning coffee at the table. After several minutes had passed, John's grandfather told him that he had killed the Dark Walker. John's mother said the matter was closed, and as a family they never spoke of it again. John's grandfather died in 1962 and John eventually moved away and raised a family of his own. John frequently returned to the hills of Aleppo Township, but never again heard the howl of the Dark Walker.

One sighting of a large and furry bipedal creature places Bigfoot close to the Greene County Airport along Rte. 21 on the night of April 18, 2015. The encounter as described doesn't have many details, only that something that looked like Bigfoot was seen walking near the interchange with I-79. What makes this report remarkable is the fact that Sasquatch was strolling very near the motel where Rosemary Ellen Guiley, in Greene

County for the weekend, had just settled in for a well-deserved rest. Who knows, perhaps Bigfoot was out searching for proof beyond the shadow of a doubt that Rosemary existed and was indeed real.

CHAPTER 16

WINGED HUMANOIDS AND DOGMEN

In recent years, researchers have received an increasing number of reports concerning unusual humanoids that appear to be half human and half animal, unknown creature or insect. The most famous is the winged humanoid Mothman of Point Pleasant, West Virginia. On November 12, 1966, five men who were digging a grave at a cemetery near Clendenin, West Virginia, claimed to see a man-like figure fly low from the trees over their heads. This was the first known sighting of what became known as the Mothman, a winged humanoid with red eyes who made numerous appearances over the next 13 months.

Shortly thereafter, on November 15, 1966, two young couples from Point Pleasant, Roger and Linda Scarberry and Steve and Mary Mallette, told police they saw a large creature whose eyes "glowed red" when the car headlights picked it up. They described it as a "large flying man with ten-foot wings" that followed their car while they were driving in an area outside of town known as "the TNT area," the site of a former World War II munitions plant. During the next few days, other people reported similar sightings.

Mothman was not the only high strangeness to plague Point Pleasant and the mid-Ohio River Valley. There was an onset of UFO activity, landed craft, encounters with aliens, poltergeist phenomena, Men In Black, and other oddities. On December 15, 1967 the Silver Bridge spanning the Ohio River at Point Pleasant collapsed, sending 46 people to their deaths. The "Mothman wave" of unusual activity came to an end. Due to a report that Mothman was seen near the bridge prior to its collapse, some believe that the creature had something to do with the tragedy.

Winged humanoids have been reported in many locations throughout history, but up until Mothman, there had never been such an intense period of unexplained activity. In 2017, a wave of winged humanoid sightings began in the Chicago area.

The Greene County winged humanoid

There is one report of a winged humanoid sighted in Greene County. In July of 2009, a lone witness was driving home at dusk along a narrow road in Wayne Township at a slow speed due to the pelting rain of a severe thunderstorm. He caught a glimpse of what he thought was a large blue heron alongside the road and slowed to a crawl to avoid hitting it. Looking closely, he realized that illuminated in his headlights was a gray humanoid figure, now standing on top of a fence post. It was easily six to seven feet tall and slender. Its skin appeared smooth and tight. It was winged, with arms at its sides.

As his vehicle drifted forward, the witness continued to stare incredulously at the figure. Still illuminated by frequent lightning, the creature was now directly beside the driver's door no more than 15 feet away – but it ignored the vehicle. It faced north and remained motionless. Its head was tapered or slightly pointed, as if it wore some type of helmet. Its wings were folded behind it with the tips pointing

Winged humanoid seen standing atop a fence post. Credit: John Weaver.

toward the ground. The eyes were very large, teardrop shaped, and black; no ears, mouth or nose were observed. Frozen with fear for what seemed like an eternity, the witness regained his composure and drove away as quickly as he could.

145

Dogmen

Another mysterious creature lurking about is the dogman. Dogmen are seen in remote forested areas, but on occasion they have been sighted in urban areas. They are often mistakenly called werewolves, but they are not humans who transform into wolves – they are unknown entities who have a body that is a mix of human and wolf or canine features. Usually they are described as having a muscular male-like torso and arms that end in wolf paws. Their heads are wolf-like, as are their legs. They can stand upright and run either on all fours or on their hind legs.

Dogmen are six to eight feet in height when standing upright on their hind legs; when on all fours they are four to five feet tall at the shoulder. Their ears are usually cropped like a Doberman's. Estimates of their weight average 400-500 pounds. They are usually accompanied by bad odors resembling rotting meat, urine, garbage or decaying hay.

Witnesses are divided as to whether dogmen are supernatural or flesh-and-blood creatures. They do not behave like physical creatures – they can disappear and appear in a flash and run too fast for ordinary creatures. People who encounter them say they have a sense they are extremely intelligent and could easily destroy a person if they chose to do so.

Dogmen have been reported in many states throughout history, and in western Pennsylvania since the 1960s. Michigan is "dogman central" with the most sightings and lore. The creatures have been seen since 1794 and are said to appear in 10-year-cycles. One of the earliest documented encounters occurred in Wexford County, Michigan in 1887. The creature was described as seven feet tall with blue or amber eyes. It was bipedal but canine-like, with the torso of a man, and it let loose a fearsome howl that sounded like a human scream.

Many dogmen have been documented in Wisconsin too; the most famous in "the Beast of Bray Road," named for a lonely county road that it seems to frequent.

Dog Boy

Closer to home in Pennsylvania, Mercer County has been a hotbed of dogman activity. In the late 1950s to early 1960s, the legend of the Shenango Valley Dog Boy sprang up around numerous reports of loud screams and howls emanating from an abandoned dairy farm on Harper Road in Jefferson Township. The Dog Boy is alleged to have been summoned by a coven of witches who once either lived in or made use of the house on that farm. They summoned Dog Boy to chase off unwanted visitors.

Two sisters, Jane and Marge, grew up not far from the farm and were told the Dog Boy story by their mother. Jane was curious and wanted to see Dog Boy but her mother ordered her to stay away from the area he supposedly protected. Jane, Marge and a friend ignored the warning and set out to find the Dog Boy one October evening. Their friend, fearing parental punishment, returned home, leaving the two sisters to continue their quest.

Their efforts were not in vain. As they approached the farm homestead there was Dog Boy crouching in the yard. His body was a mixture of human and canine features, and one arm seemed to be deformed. Covered in dark brown or black hair, Dog Boy was 3 to 4 feet tall at the shoulder when crouching on all four feet.

Terrified, the sisters ran home and told their mother about their encounter. A few nights later, the two sisters, along with their mother and some other friends, returned to the area. As they approached the milk house they heard a high-pitched howl. Jane and Marge's mother shouted instructions for the girls to run back the way they had come. Marge was the youngest and shortest in the group and was easily outdistanced by the others.

Dog Boy was able to overtake Marge and grab her left hand. Her mother, realizing Marge had fallen behind, looked over her shoulder to see Marge struggling to break free of Dog Boy's grip. Coming to her aid, her mother seized her right hand and a terrifying tug of war ensued between mother, daughter, and Dog Boy. Dog Boy lost his grip and retreated into the darkness, allowing Marge and her mother to escape unharmed. During 1990-1991, Dog Boy returned to the area, and he was sighted again in 2014.

The Wild Dog Man

There have been at least two sightings of dogmen in Greene County. While both were terrifying to the eyewitnesses, one of the mysterious encounters has been solved. In 1987, a doe hunter parked his truck along the Washington-Greene County line and made his way through the woods to his tree stand. Hoping to spot deer, he heard some rustling in the leaves and watched intently. What he saw was a creature with canine features running upright like a human. It stopped briefly and sniffed the air, then quickly ran off. The hunter, frozen with fear, sat in his tree stand for several hours. He climbed down at midday, quickly returned to his parked vehicle and left the area. He immediately retired from hunting and has not been in the woods since.

In July of 1930 there was a series of reports from the Mapletown, Carmichaels and Greensboro areas of Greene County regarding a Dogman or Wild Dog Man. The reports were so sensational they even appeared in the *Pittsburgh Post-Gazette*, where this story was found.

Numerous eyewitnesses reported sighting a disheveled, nearly naked Wild Dog Man frequenting the wooded areas near Mapletown and Carmichaels. The Wild Dog Man made bizarre, unintelligible sounds as he crawled about on four feet like a dog. Several eyewitnesses reported sighting the Wild Dog Man to the local authorities, and one motorist claimed to have threatened the bizarre man-animal with a wrench while parked near the Masontown Bridge.

All the eyewitnesses were in agreement that there was some form of a wild man/dog man in the area who was nearly naked and hopped about on four feet, and when confronted would run back into the woods. Taking the reports seriously, local law enforcement officials, along with members of the Pennsylvania State Police, were mobilized and launched a manhunt to find and subdue the Wild Dog Man.

In what perhaps is the only Dogman case ever solved, the lawmen, accompanied by the *Post-Gazette's* Joe Shuman, did in fact locate the Wild Dog Man chopping wood at his family's farm near Mapletown. As it turned out, the Wild Dog Man was a partially handicapped young man of about 17 years of age named Clyde. The youth, who not only had suffered from polio but may have been illiterate and developmentally disabled as well, was described by his mother as "ain't right smart." Clyde's family looked after him as best they could, and he did routine chores around the homestead.

They owned a few cattle, and one named Billy decided he preferred freedom to the confines of his pasture and barn. Clyde attempted to prevent Billy's wanderings by latching onto Billy's halter, which prompted the bovine to run off. At this point, Clyde either panicked or was determined not to let Billy roam free. In either case, he did not loosen his grip on the halter.

Undeterred, Billy took Clyde for the ride, or rather drag, of his life across the fields and through the woods. Clyde lost his shoes, his hat, and most of his clothing in the process. By the time he either let go or Billy finally broke free, the young lad, who had never been away from home before, was totally lost. Battered, beaten, bruised, no doubt covered in scrapes and scratches, hatless, shoeless, nearly naked, possibly bloody and swollen, poor Clyde was frightening people as he approached them no doubt in a vain attempt to obtain help in finding his way home.

While the fate of Billy the Bovine is unknown, luckily Clyde's grandfather found him wandering in the woods alone at 1 AM one morning and took him home, where the local constabulary and the newspaper reporter found him that warm July afternoon in 1930.

CHAPTER 17

ANGRY SPIRITS OF THE LAND

Out in the hills beyond Wayne Township, a small farm sat abandoned for a good number of years. The small two-story farmhouse, built in the early 19th century, was in disrepair and had never been updated with indoor plumbing. The weed-choked fields were bordered on three sides by forest. Underneath the land was a honeycomb of abandoned mine tunnels.

In the mid-2000s, the land was purchased with the intent of reinvigorating the farm, and a manager, a local agricultural man, was hired for the makeover. But when Jack (not his real name) set to work on the property, he discovered that some unexpected "bonuses" came with the land: ghosts of dead people, a poltergeist, a cat-like imp creature, shadow people, alien-looking beings, phantom creatures with too many legs – and "It," a powerful entity of unknown origins with shapeshifting ability and a nasty attitude. In short order, It put out a "You Are Not Welcome" sign.

151

The farm sat in ideal territory for mysterious activity. It was remote and unattended. In paranormal lore, mine tunnels, wells, springs and other subterranean openings to the surface provide excellent corridors for spirit travel.

Jack had lived all of his life in the area around the farm, and he was at home in country ways and life. Odd things happen and are seen out in the woods, and Jack was used to that. Things were "out there" that you just didn't talk about.

From the very first, Jack knew there was something very peculiar about the farm. It had an "atmosphere." He shrugged it off.

There was much to be done: clear the brush, plant gardens, get coops up for chickens, repair the house. As soon as Jack and volunteers got busy, a heavy, oppressive feeling of being watched pervaded the property. What was more, whatever was watching did not seem to be friendly.

The first hint of something seriously askew happened one winter day while Jack was ripping down the old curtains inside the farmhouse. The oppressive feeling of being watched was worse than usual, making him uncomfortable. He began seeing strange flashes of light across the ceiling, as though someone were flashing a camera. Then he glanced out a window and saw something that made his skin crawl.

Peering through the glass was a creature unlike anything known on Earth. Its head, neck and a suggestion of shoulders were visible. The head resembled the grotesque caricature of a hairless cat, with pointed ears set way back, big yellow eyes with vertical slits, crooked cat-like teeth protruding from its closed mouth, and dark brown, leathery skin. It looked frail and spindly. If standing, it would have been about three-and-a-half feet tall.

Fear shot through Jack. Impulsively, he shouted out, "In the name of Jesus Christ, get thee behind me!" It was the first time in his life he had ever invoked the Lord's name against anything. Whatever the thing was, it felt evil.

152

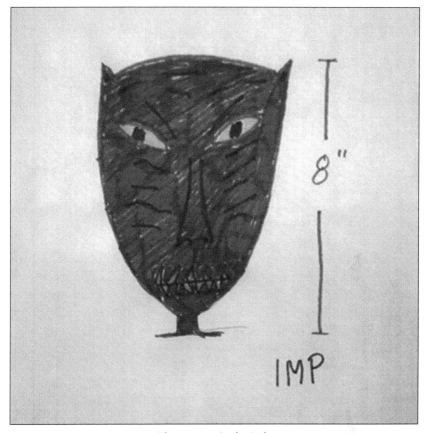

The imp cat. Credit: Jack.

The creature vanished, but not for good. It showed up again.

Rattled, Jack contacted a friend of his who was a Presbyterian minister. The minister was convinced the creature was a demon, but Jack disagreed. It didn't seem like a demon, but he did not know what it was. "What they teach you in Sunday school doesn't even come close to everything that's out there," he told his friend.

Sometime after that, Jack was perusing books to see if he could find a likeness of the creature. He came across a woodcut drawing of a medieval demon, an imp-like creature that was called a guardian of the woodlands.

Had something been rustled out of the woods by all the clearing and activity?

The imp, as Jack liked to call the creature, was only the opening act for much more to follow.

The farmhouse was not suitable for living, and Jack used it as an office, storage facility and resting area; the downstairs had a kitchen table, some furniture, and a pellet stove. It did have a landline telephone; there was no cellphone service in the area.

Jack never stayed all night there but went home to his own place in a neighboring town. In the mornings, he would open up the locked house and sometimes find things in disarray. The phone would be taken apart, the batteries out, and all the pieces left lying on the desk. The window where the imp cat had appeared would be jimmied open, and muddy creature-like footprints would be found on the windowsill and floor. Objects, especially tools, would go missing and turn up in odd locations. Human-like footprints with impressions of a long skirt dragging behind them were found upstairs, where the two empty bedrooms seemed to harbor a lot of unusual activity.

In the entire house, the upstairs felt the worst in "atmosphere." Sometimes Jack could feel a presence moving around the house, and it would zip upstairs, where he felt it hid in a closet. Thumping, banging, footsteps, the sounds of heavy objects being dragged across the floor, the sound of small objects like marbles being dropped on the floor and the sound of a large object like a bowling ball being dropped were heard when no living person was upstairs. Sometimes he saw out of the corner of his eye dark shadow forms flitting about.

One day an open house was being held at the farm, and the thumping and banging was particularly annoying. Jack went upstairs to the bedroom where he felt "things" hid in the closet. He remembered the advice of his Presbyterian minister friend: "Don't ever invoke the name of the Lord and tell something to go without giving it a destination," the friend had said.

In a loud and forceful voice, Jack invoked the Lord and said, "You go do your thumping and banging at the Lord's feet because I've got too much to do here to mess with you."

The noises stopped. They returned from time to time, but never at the same volume.

In the summertime, student volunteers would help out with chores. It seemed they, too, felt there was something present that they needed to defend themselves against. One intern showed up with a 9mm pistol strapped to his hip.

"What are you doing with that gun?" Jack asked him, alarmed.

"I have a permit for it," the young man replied.

"That's not what I asked you. Are you going to shoot groundhogs?"

"No," the intern said. "I swear there are people in the house when nobody is supposed to be there, and I want to be able to defend myself when I have to go in alone."

"It's not going to do you any good, so put it back in the car," Jack said. "All you are going to do is shoot a hole in the house and tick me off."

Another intern was a devout young man who brought his Bible to work and read it every day while he ate lunch in the kitchen. You could tell his Bible was a treasured possession, for he kept it in a nice leather cover. He did not believe in the paranormal.

One day Jack walked into the house while the intern was eating and reading. The young man looked at him and turned pale white. "I thought you were upstairs," he said in a shaky voice to Jack. "There are footsteps up there, someone walking around."

Jack shook his head. "I've been outside all day," he said.

There was no one else on the property. After that, the intern read his Bible more furiously than ever. Soon he was gone.

Jack got introduced to the ghosts on the property. One day he was outside the farmhouse on an extension ladder working on the exterior near one of the upper floor bedroom windows. Looking in, he was greeted by a heavyset, stern woman staring at him – and she did not look at all happy to see him. Jack almost fell off the ladder.

The woman may have been a former occupant of the house. Curious, Jack did some research on the house's history, and found references to a woman whose baby died in the house at age one month. Phantom sounds of a baby crying were supposed to be heard around the anniversary of the infant's death.

More pervasive was a ghost Jack nicknamed Porter, after another former human resident, long since deceased. Porter glided around the outside, a tall, skinny dark shadow figure wearing a ball cap and overalls. He seemed intensely interested in anything to do with machinery, and sometimes peered over Jack's shoulder while he was operating something. His presence was unnerving but not threatening.

Other phantoms were more animal-like. The house was occupied by "little gray scurrying things," creatures that were light gray, about the size of tailless cats, and had many legs. They scurried along the baseboards and up and down the stairs.

Jack captured some peculiar images with his camera when he photographed one of the upstairs bedroom windows. He felt watched from the house so often when he was outside that he started carrying his camera with him all the time. One day when the feeling came over him,

Cat-headed creature looks out an upper window. Outline shows small figure, perhaps a doll, held by creature. Photo is reproduced to the right. Credit: Jack.

he snapped a shot of the window, even though he could not physically see anything in it.

The photograph revealed a chilling image. Looking out and down at him was a large, pale figure with a distorted face and a leering, saw-toothed grin. It had cat-like ears on top of its head.

There was a mystery visitor as well, a man – or was it something else masquerading as a man? Jack was outside working one afternoon when a shiny, black late model Ford pickup turned off the dirt road into the driveway of the farm. The road down the hollow is long and dusty. In spite of the dust, the truck was spotless, as though it had just come fresh out of a car wash. A gray-haired, middle-aged man who looked like "Joe Average" leaned out of the open window. "Say, did you ever know O____ K____?" he hailed at Jack. O.K. was a former owner of the place, now deceased. Jack replied that he did not.

"Boy, he was a character," the stranger said. "I should stop and tell you about him sometime." And with that he backed up and drove off.

Jack had no clue who the stranger was. But he came by two more times, in the same spotless black Ford pickup. He always said the same thing and then drove off. Jack never saw the man or the truck anywhere else in the area.

After the third visit, Jack resolved to invite the man inside the house and take his photograph. Sure enough, the stranger came again. "Say, did you ever know O____ K____?" he said to Jack.

"No," Jack replied. "But why don't you come inside the house and tell me about him? I'd like to take your picture, too."

The stranger stared at him. "No," he said flatly. He backed up his truck and drove off, never to return again.

If the activity had stopped there with ghosts, poltergeists, mysterious sounds, a peculiar visitor and even an imp cat, Jack might have chalked up the farm to an extremely haunted house in a haunted hollow. There was something else going on, however, that indicated a deeper mystery.

Stray farm cats are not unusual in the country. They come and go. For a time, the farm had several, including one given as a gift by a volunteer student. One day the student was coming to visit, and her tabby cat was nowhere to be seen. Jack went looking for it – and made a grisly discovery inside the house. Opening the door to a storage room, Jack found the remains of the tabby. It had been slit open and all of its soft tissue had been removed. The bones, muscle and pelt remained. There was not a drop of blood or bloodstains anywhere. The gutting was so clean that the remains could have been donned as a bizarre hat. Jack took the remains outside and left them on the hill. After the student left, he went to fetch the carcass to bury it – but it had vanished.

The tabby was the only cat ever mutilated at the farm. Occasionally, some of the chickens would be found dead inside their pens, not mangled or partially devoured as one might expect from a natural predator attack. There were never any clues as to what had killed them. The pens were behind an electrified fence.

Sometimes the dead chickens would be lined up neatly inside the pens. An animal predator, of course, would have left a mangled mess or carted them off.

Jack installed a motion sensor camera to discover what was preying upon the chickens. Nothing ever showed up – and chickens continued to die.

The hillside had its own peculiar haunting energy. Jack began to experience that a certain patch of the hill was always trouble. If he drove his pickup through it, or operated machinery in it, there was always a breakdown. He felt strange passing through the patch. He called it "The Forbidden Zone."

Finally, out on the hillside, Jack met a force or an entity that seemed very powerful and very intelligent. And it did not like him.

It usually showed itself as a gray or dark form that moved swiftly over the ground or wove through the trees. Sometimes it was a ball. Once he saw it as a flat rug that rolled itself up into a ball. As it moved and picked up speed, it changed shape, from a ball to a flattened oval. He could watch it for up to about 10 seconds, and then it would vanish into thin air, or seem to drop into the ground and disappear. In addition, there were colored balls of light that bobbed around over the ground.

Jack felt that It was the presence that watched him in a hostile fashion. As time went on, It was able to communicate through Jack's thoughts that he was unwelcome there – in fact, all people were unwelcome. The land belonged to It, and It wanted him to GET OUT.

The longer Jack worked at the farm, the stronger these impressions became, and the more intense the paranormal activity became. There would be waves of activity followed by troughs of relative quiet. It seemed to be able to get into his head, plant negative and depressing thoughts, and affect his mood. He suffered minor but strange injuries and annoying health issues that defied explanation. He developed a reluctance to go into the woods alone.

The activity followed Jack home as well. One night, driving home on the lonely road through heavy rain punctuated with thunder and lightning, Jack saw a dark, menacing figure sitting on a fence post, illuminated for a few seconds by a flash of lightning. It stared at him with heavy dark eyes and seemed to be waiting for him to pass by.

Jack's home was affected with poltergeist and phantom activity – the little gray scurrying things, and a fast-moving creature with mole-like claws that attacked him in bed. He started sleeping downstairs with the lights and the TV on. His family experienced phenomena, too.

Having heard about Rosemary and her paranormal investigations, Jack contacted her with a request to visit and sort out what in the paranormal blazes was going on at the farm. Curious to find out why such a little piece of land seemed to be such a hotbed of paranormal activity, she agreed.

Rosemary and Kevin contacted some paranormal investigator friends in Pennsylvania to arrange for some surveillance, and to see what evidence might be captured. From the start, they experienced what became a pattern. There would be intense activity such as shadow forms and noises from early evening to about 1 AM, and then nothing for the remainder of the night.

And, every investigation was marred by a sudden health issue that prevented someone on the team from participating or forcing a cancellation. Everyone but Rosemary was affected in this manner.

The worst and most alarming attack affected Jack. On the eve of an investigation day and evening, Jack was rushed to the hospital with signs of a possible heart attack. He was all right and soon back on his feet – but investigations had to be tabled for some time.

Instead of health problems, Rosemary was plagued with car breakdowns. Something obviously did not want anyone poking around.

All the investigations were plagued with difficulties with equipment – cameras turned off by themselves, batteries failed, recorders stopped working, and so on. While the investigators witnessed phenomena such as shadow forms, the little gray scurrying things, Porter and the imp cat, they were never able to capture anything in a photo or on video. Whatever was there was deliberately elusive.

Investigations were conducted during the day as well. Out on the hillside, the air would suddenly thicken in a strange way, and a presence could be felt that was surely It. As It moved around, the air would ripple. It resembled the rippling air that marked the alien in the *Predator* films.

One night, a large and overpowering shadow man came into the house during an investigation. Everyone saw it as it darted about the room, suddenly here, suddenly there, up the stairs, down the stairs. Everyone felt nauseated in its presence. It settled into a corner and seemed to glower at the group, though no facial features were visible.

"You will not touch any of us," Rosemary told it.

The shadow man made no move toward anyone in the group; however, the group later discovered that all the surveillance equipment stopped working at that time, simultaneously. It was as though the shadow person had made a point – maybe it would not touch us, but our equipment was not off limits.

On another occasion, the investigators arranged for an all-nighter. Jack did not participate, but asked Rosemary to call him on the landline by midnight to let him know everyone was all right.

The shadow man was present again early in the evening, and a weird atmosphere filled the house. Thumping sounded upstairs. When Rosemary tried to call Jack at the appointed time, the phone malfunctioned and then went dead. The investigators felt completely isolated.

Then they could not get the door to the outside open. It was as though the door were bolted shut internally. They tugged and pulled and could not budge it open. It seemed straight out of Hollywood – the evil house that warns people to get out, and then bolts all the doors shut on them. They contemplated breaking windows – and then suddenly the door sprang open.

Soon none of the other investigators were available to continue at the farm, as though they had been removed from the case.

Events then took an interesting turn when Jack introduced Rosemary to Gayle (not her real name). Gayle had been to the farm and felt she could communicate with It. She also felt that It visited her in her home miles away, causing some of the same effects it did at the farm, as well as attacking her at night. Once Gayle felt a form behind her in bed. She reached back – and connected with something solid that felt like a combination of clammy skin and a mole-like foot. She turned and glanced at it, catching a flash of brown before it disappeared. Was it the same mole-like entity that had attacked Jack?

A devout woman, Gayle relied heavily on prayer – especially the Lord's Prayer – and reciting scripture in order to banish unwanted presences. For a long time, she kept a Bible underneath her mattress for fast and easy access. One day it vanished without explanation or trace. At the time of her meeting with Rosemary, it had been missing for about a year.

Gayle had a long history of paranormal encounters going back to childhood. As a young girl, she was often held prisoner by an invisible presence that locked her bedroom door to prevent her from leaving. When it decided to let her out, the door would open. She also had seen shadows and apparitions and had experienced a host of paranormal phenomena.

162

Despite the unsettling events at the farm, Gayle had no fear of going there, or of It. She felt connected to the place and was very familiar with it from her first visit. Once she was visiting there, eating pizza with several other people at the kitchen table. Suddenly the sound of a tinny music box – the old-fashioned kind with tines on a roller – wafted through the air. There was no such music box on site, of course – and no radio or television, either.

When Gayle entered the picture, Rosemary began having coin materializations – pennies, nickels and dimes that mysteriously appeared in odd places in her home and in hotel rooms where she stayed. Objects that appear without explanation are called "apports" in psychical research.

The coins appeared on Rosemary's furniture, fell out of clothing that had no pockets and were hanging in her closets, and showed up on carpets. All the coins were dated from the late 1950s to the 1970s, and they all were roughened, like they had been sanded or abraded.

Rosemary made arrangements to interview Gayle, and on the eve of the interview strange things happened. A 1957 penny appeared on the floor of Rosemary's hotel room. Gayle had the crowns of two front teeth fall off simultaneously, putting her in pain and forcing her to cancel the interview. Her dentist was at a loss to explain why the crowns fell off, especially two of them at the same time.

Rosemary and Gayle were finally able to meet, however. Rosemary learned that Gayle had been having penny apports for years in connection with It and had filled jars with them. On the same night that Rosemary had the 1957 penny apport, Gayle had also had a 1957 penny apport. Something was watching and wanted them to know.

We had not been able to get It to communicate much, except with threatening impressions, and we asked Gayle if she would be willing to make contact. Gayle had never done any channeling or mediumship, nor had she ever participated in a séance. She agreed, and had no fear of doing so, because, she said, It wanted to speak through her to make certain things known. Rosemary set up a séance at the farm, attended by her, Gayle, Jack, and several others who were paranormal colleagues.

The séance took place on a gray, rainy night, done in candlelit darkness in the living room of the farmhouse. After invoking protection, Rosemary asked for the entity to answer our questions via Gayle. She did not go into a trance but spoke the words that came into her mind.

The entity told us that it was ancient and had lived "beneath the Earth" in that area for a very long time, longer than people had been around. The place we called "the farm," as well as a large chunk of land beyond it, belonged to the entity, and it did not like people living or working there. It had a low regard of humans and wished to be left alone. It was angry that humans had no respect.

It resented much of the activity done on the land by Jack and his volunteers, especially the mowing, clearing of the brush, and culling of trees in the woods. It detested the sound and operation of machinery. Consequently, it targeted Jack for harassment. It also pestered Gayle.

Everyone thought perhaps Jack's natural attunement to the paranormal made him an easier mark than most others who spent time on the farm. Jack had repeatedly asked It not to bother him and had stated his intention for a peaceful coexistence – but It was not interested in sharing what It considered to be rightfully its own property. An analogy might be how humans would view pests who invade their home. You don't care if the rodents or ants want to coexist with you – you just want them out of your space.

There was no reasoning with this entity. It stated flatly that it wanted everybody off the land, and it would make people miserable until they left.

Kevin suggested that one more remedy be tried. He procured a pouch of ceremonial tobacco from the local Shawnee, and he and Rosemary made a formal offering of it to the entity, sprinkling some around the farmhouse and burning some in an iron pot outside.

The offering quieted the paranormal activity, but only for a temporary period. Then it was back to waves of activity that had debilitating effects on anyone who spent much time there.

The farm is now abandoned again, and weeds choke the landscape.

How many other cases are like the farm? Our ancestors were well aware that spirits roam the landscape and claim areas as their private domain. In earlier times such areas were left untouched, out of fear of retribution if not respect. The consequences may not have been as harsh as at the farm, but nonetheless there were "understandings" that certain places were best left wild and alone.

In today's times of the bulldozer and the developer, we seldom think of any territorial lines, especially with unseen spirits – if we believe in them at all. In many cases, spirits of the land just move on when people arrive; some may haunt places for periods of time.

Every now and then, they push back – and with force.

We hope you have enjoyed the tour of some of Greene County's supernatural mysteries. This little corner of the Keystone State is full of mystery – and we've hit only the tip of it. If you have a Greene County story to share, email the authors: Kevin Paul is at hauntedgc@yahoo.com and Rosemary Ellen Guiley is at reguiley@gmail.com.

ABOUT THE AUTHORS

Rosemary Ellen Guiley

Rosemary Ellen Guiley is a bestselling author, researcher and investigator in the paranormal and related fields, including UFOs, aliens, cryptids and unknown entities and spirits. She is the author of more than 65 books.

Rosemary is the owner and president of Visionary Living, Inc. Publishing and Media, which publishes books on the paranormal, UFOs, cryptids and related topics, and also topics in the body mind spirit field.

She lectures and researches internationally and is a frequent media guest on major radio shows, including *Coast to Coast AM* with

George Noory, *The Conspiracy Show* with Richard Syrett and *Exploring Unexplained Phenomena* with Scott Colborn.

Her personal website is
www.visionaryliving.com

and her publishing house is at
www.visionarylivingpublishing.com.

Kevin Paul

A descendant of some of the prominent first European families to settle what is now modern-day Greene County, Kevin Paul was immersed at an early age in local folklore and its application to everyday life in rural southwestern Pennsylvania. His interest in studying the paranormal began when headlines about the Mothman sightings in Point Pleasant, West Virginia first appeared in local newspapers in 1966.

A graduate of West Virginia University, he has worked in sales, agricultural marketing, and conservation of natural resources. His farm background, interest in history, and study of the unexplained led to the collection of stories of high strangeness found in this book.

Currently he works to find ways to connect local farms with consumers. In his spare time, he enjoys relaxing with his wife, listening to big band music, reading, and taking leisurely drives on less traveled highways.

Bibliography

Martinez, Susan. *The Lost History of the Little People: Their Spiritually Advanced Civilizations Around the World.* New York: Inner Traditions/Bear, 2013.

Johansen, Bruce and Pritzker, Barry. Santa Barbara, CA: *Encyclopedia of American Indian History.* ABC-CLIO, 2007.

Bates, S. P. *History of Greene County Pennsylvania.* Chicago: Nelson, Rishforth and Co., 1888.

Waychoff, A. J. *Local History of Greene County and Southwestern Pennsylvania.* Waynesburg, PA: Cornerstone Genealogical Society, 1994.